SECRETS AND SPIES

INSIGHTS

CRITICAL THINKING ON INTERNATIONAL AFFAIRS

Providing new perspectives and knowledge on an increasingly complex, uncertain, and interconnected world.

The Chatham House Insights Series

Series Editor: Caroline Soper

The Insights series provides new perspectives on and knowledge about an increasingly complex, uncertain, and interconnected world. Concise, lively, and authoritative, these books explore, through different modes of interpretation, a wide range of country, regional, and international developments, all within a global context. Focusing on topical issues in key policy areas, such as health, security, economics, law, and the environment, volumes in the series will be written accessibly by leading experts—both academic and practitioner—to anticipate trends and illuminate new ideas and thinking. Insights books will be of great interest to all those seeking to develop a deeper understanding of the policy challenges and choices facing decisionmakers, including academics, practitioners, and general readers.

Published or forthcoming titles:

Amitai Etzioni, *Foreign Policy: Thinking Outside the Box* (2016)

David Lubin, *Dance of the Trillions: Developing Countries and Global Finance* (2018)

Keir Giles, *Moscow Rules: What Drives Russia to Confront the West* (2019)

Nigel Gould-Davies, *Tectonic Politics: Global Political Risk in an Age of Transformation* (2019)

Chatham House, the Royal Institute of International Affairs, is a world-leading policy institute based in London. Its mission is to help governments and societies build a sustainably secure, prosperous, and just world.

SECRETS AND SPIES

U.K. Intelligence Accountability after Iraq and Snowden

JAMIE GASKARTH

BROOKINGS INSTITUTION PRESS
Washington, D.C.

CHATHAM HOUSE
The Royal Institute of International Affairs
London

1775 Massachusetts Avenue, N.W., Washington, D.C. 20036
www.brookings.edu

Library of Congress Cataloging-in-Publication Data.
Names: Gaskarth, Jamie, 1976– author.
Title: Secrets and spies : UK intelligence accountability
after Iraq and Snowden / Jamie Gaskarth.
Description: Washington, D.C. : Brookings Institution Press, [2020] | Series: The Chatham House insights series | Includes bibliographical references and index.
Identifiers: LCCN 2019048135 (print) | LCCN 2019048136 (ebook) | ISBN 9780815737971 (paperback : alk. paper) | ISBN 9780815737988 (epub)
Subjects: LCSH: Intelligence service—Great Britain—History—21st century. | Government accountability—Great Britain—History—21st century.
Classification: LCC JN329.I6 G37 2020 (print) | LCC JN329.I6 (ebook) | DDC 327.1241—dc23
LC record available at https://lccn.loc.gov/2019048135
LC ebook record available at https://lccn.loc.gov/2019048136

9 8 7 6 5 4 3 2 1

Typeset in Adobe Garamond

Composition by Elliott Beard

Contents

Acknowledgments

First, I would like to express my thanks for Caroline Soper's encouragement and intellectual input in making this book a reality. Caroline is a brilliant editor of International Affairs and has continued to be an inspiration as Insights Series editor. I am also grateful to Amanda Moss of Chatham House and Bill Finan, Kristen Harrison, and Cecilia González of the Brookings Institution Press for all their help and support, as well as Olga Gardner Galvin for her attentive copyediting skills.

I conducted over forty interviews, discussions, coffees, and lunches with former and current intelligence practitioners as well as members of the ISC and IPCO, former foreign secretaries and ministers, and other interested parties. It is unfortunate that I cannot name them, for obvious reasons, but the project would not have been possible without them generously giving up their time and wisdom. I am very thankful to the British Academy for awarding me a research grant that enabled this project to happen in the first place (SG151249). I have also benefited from the kindness of academic colleagues who read drafts or offered insights into the intelligence world. Special thanks go to Rory Cormac, Steve Hewitt, Scott Lucas, Adam Quinn, Tim Edmunds, Frank Foley, Raquel Da Silva, Richard Aldrich, Abigail

Watson, Nicholas Kitchen, as well as Nichola Hardwicke for her brilliant transcription skills and Ben Whale and Jessica Rowley for their diligent research assistance. Any opinions or errors in the text are, of course, my own. The University of Birmingham has generously provided support for conference attendance and offered an intellectual environment for developing my ideas, which is much appreciated. Thanks also to my wife, Ellie, and daughters, Marla and Peggy, for keeping me sane and distracted. Above all, it is Joanna and John Luxford and Michael and Teresa Connolly who made this book possible through their heroic childcare efforts. I therefore dedicate it to them with love.

Introduction

In 2017, a series of terrorist attacks in London and Manchester killed thirty-six innocent people and injured nearly two hundred others. Three of the six attackers were known to the British Security Service, two of them having previously been subjects of interest and one, Khuram Butt, the subject of an active investigation. Indeed, Butt was under surveillance and footage was recorded of him loading the van that would eventually be used to kill two people on London Bridge before the attackers went on to murder a further six people. The partner of one of the victims expressed shock on hearing this information, arguing, "It's important the authorities know that society, including the victim's families, will hold them accountable for any errors."[1]

This begs the question: what does accountability mean in this context? After these attacks, the home secretary ordered a series of internal reviews by police forces and the Security Service to identify areas for operational improvement. The nine classified reports that resulted were themselves reviewed by Sir David Anderson, QC,[2] and the unclassified version of his report was released to the public in December 2017.[3] The Intelligence and Security Committee (ISC) also produced a report on these attacks to set out what needed to change.[4] In addition, the inquests included cross-examination of security personnel and investigation into procedures connected with monitoring suspects. If accountability means giving an account of one's actions, then these agencies did so extensively, both within their organizations and externally to oversight bodies and the wider public. Lessons were learned, with the classified reports detailing 126 recommendations for changes to future practice.

However, if accountability means identifying culpability and highlighting errors, that is more problematic. Anderson explicitly refused to apportion blame. When it came to judgments about the closing of surveillance, the reviews concluded that the decisions were "sound on the basis of the available information at the time."[5] Despite noting that, in the case of the Manchester attacks, the decision to close an investigation on the perpetrator was "wrong," Anderson argued: "Substantial and appropriate coverage was in place around key individuals, and mechanisms designed to assess risk were working as intended."[6] Rather than individual or systemic failings, he concluded that "MI5 and CT Policing got a great deal right . . . they could have succeeded had the cards fallen differently."[7] Thus, failure came down to chance.

Critics of intelligence accountability in the United Kingdom have seen this tendency in other reviews.[8] Since 9/11, a series of inquiries have been conducted into the work of the intelligence and security agencies. These were prompted either by allegations of poor performance (for instance, in assessing Iraq's WMD capabilities prior to the 2003 war, or failing to prevent the murder of a soldier, Lee Rigby, in 2013, and the 2017 attacks) or impropriety (such as involvement in rendition, mistreatment of detainees in the war on terror, or mass surveillance of British citizens without legal authority). The reports often conclude that errors would not have made a difference to outcomes, avoid apportioning blame to individuals, and ascribe mistakes to faulty systems and processes.[9] In many instances, news commentary refutes the findings, arguing that vital evidence was missed or that the inquiries were misled.[10]

For some, this suggests that intelligence accountability in the United Kingdom is deeply flawed. By their logic, the intelligence and security agencies have seen massive increases in resources and budgets yet have continued to make mistakes, miss new security developments, and act illegally and unethically without consequences.[11] An alternative view would note that mistakes have been brought to light, officials have been compelled to give an account of their behavior, and changes have been made internally within these organizations as well as externally, to the regulatory framework under which they operate. Thus, in many ways, the discussion is polarized between those who question the purpose of these agencies and their role in government, and those who feel that they are operating effectively and should largely be left to carry on with their work.[12]

This book sets out to address this debate and explore how accountability functions in relation to the U.K. secret intelligence and security agencies. Holding these agencies to account is important for a number of reasons. Globally, Britain is plugged into networks, like the "Five Eyes" arrangement with the United States, Canada, Australia, and New Zealand, that produce intelligence used to inform and even define international responses to crises such as Iraq (1990–2003), Libya (2011), Syria (2011–ongoing), and Ukraine (2014–ongoing). As such, they play a vital role in providing the evidence basis for international decisionmaking; however, the flip side of this is that if the U.K. agencies make errors and share faulty intelligence, it can have global implications—most clearly in the case of the buildup to the war in Iraq in 2003. In addition to bad policy outcomes, mistakes can lead to reputational damage for the British state. Furthermore, allegations of U.K. impropriety over rendition, the treatment of detainees overseas, and surveillance are significant, as they legitimize negative behavior among liaison partners, some of whom may have poor human rights records. Thus they can affect Britain's wider normative goals as well as global human rights standards.

Nationally, the most important features of the performance of Britain's secret agencies are how far they are able to keep British citizens safe and to what extent they offer reliable intelligence to inform policymaking.[13] The record on these counts is mixed. The director general of the Security Service, Andrew Parker, asserted in October 2017 that "Twenty attacks had been foiled in the last four years, including seven in the last seven months" and saw the threat from terrorism as "at the highest tempo I have seen in my 34-year career."[14] Although the number of foiled plots increased, so did the number of successful attacks, with a spike of five being carried out in 2017. Moreover, the overwhelming attention paid to terrorism raised concerns in the Intelligence and Security Committee that other threats, such as hostile state activity and foreign espionage, were not being given sufficient weight.[15] With the poisoning of Sergei Skripal and four other people in Salisbury in 2018, including the death of Dawn Sturgess, attention was drawn to a series of suspicious deaths of British citizens and Russian émigrés over the previous decade, which were argued to have not been given the attention they deserved.[16] According to Duncan Allen, "The Salisbury attack was not just a brazen violation of U.K. sovereignty. It was also a U.K. policy failure: the failure, again, to protect a U.K. national from attacks by organs of the Russian state."[17]

In terms of reliable intelligence, the shadow of Iraq hangs over much of the public impression of these agencies, but arguably not enough has been made of the lack of warning of the Taliban uprising in Helmand Province, Afghanistan, in 2006; the Arab Spring in 2011; or the rise of Islamic State in 2014 (see chapter 2). It will be argued later that the agencies seem to respond well to crises but are poor at anticipating them in the first place. This is an area that often gets little attention in accountability circles but has major consequences for security and defense policy.[18]

Furthermore, there have been some notable operational errors based on faulty intelligence, which have had repercussions. In the most serious cases, mistakes have led to innocent people being shot and killed,[19] wrongful arrests, and families broken up, with children taken into the care system unnecessarily.[20] The agencies might counter that they operate under an unprecedented level of scrutiny and regulation, and such faults are rare. Yet, as this book will demonstrate, some of these problems persist despite warnings from external scrutiny bodies and commissioners about procedural failings that contributed to outcomes.

Beyond these performance issues, the activities of the intelligence and security agencies have ethical repercussions for governance, the relationship between citizens and the state, and community cohesion.[21] As Anthony Glees and Philip Davies put it: "Intelligence and security matters impact more deeply on our nation's life, now at war and also at peace, and on its security and well-being, than almost any other matters. They affect the very nature of our government and the policies that it pursues."[22] Efforts to deter radicalization, such as the PREVENT program, have been controversial in target communities, which feel demonized and implicitly blamed for the actions of a minority of individuals.[23] Yet the U.K. agencies have responded to criticism, and coupled with the civilian and cooperative nature of their work in this area, this means that they have arguably managed to deal with the issue of radicalization in a less confrontational way than some other countries.[24] The fact that the United Kingdom enjoys relative harmony in its domestic affairs both informs the agencies' approach and is also an effect of their efforts to act with the consent and goodwill of the general public.

When it comes to appraising the work of the agencies, commentators tend to focus on one or more of the following three aspects of their functioning: their effectiveness, their efficiency, and their ethics.[25] Analyzing these facets of their operation can bring benefits to the agencies themselves as well as the government and society they serve. Organizations that are not subject to rigorous accountability mechanisms risk tying themselves to outdated thinking and practices out of habit.[26] Samuel Rascoff has argued that "without appropriately scaled and designed governance, intelligence is likely to become nonrigorous and ultimately ineffective at providing policymakers with the informational advantage they need to keep terrorist threats at bay."[27] Proper scrutiny can provide a useful check on whether policy is ethical and procedures are robust enough to serve political goals. Moreover, ineffective accountability makes it difficult to identify and challenge individuals who are undermining organizational norms or goals for personal reasons.[28] Secrecy and access to information offer the individuals who work for these agencies considerable power. It is inevitable that some will seek to use this for their personal advantage. Such instances appear to be rare in the United Kingdom, but accountability mechanisms provide important ways of exposing their behavior and suggesting procedures to minimize the chances of such people having access to sensitive material in the future. Thus, it is in the agencies' own interest to have their assumptions challenged and their behavior scrutinized so that they can challenge poor policies, root out bad apples, receive new and innovative ideas, and be confident they are operating effectively.

In addition to these practical concerns, exploration of accountability with regard to the U.K. secret agencies is worth studying, as it has implications for academic debates in public policy and governance. Secrecy presents a challenge for accountability, because giving an account requires sharing information—a process that could undermine the very function of these agencies. Theories of accountability tend to be predicated on the liberal assumptions that open argumentation, wider participation, public dissemination of knowledge, institutionalization, and regulation improve public policy.[29] If Britain's secret agencies are able to function effectively, maintain their efficiency, and resist the corrupting influence of unchecked power, despite a limited regulatory environment and the constraints of secrecy, then this may challenge these preconceptions.

In short, it is vital to analyze intelligence accountability in the United Kingdom, because the activities of Britain's intelligence and security agencies have important international and national effects. The analysis also has implications for academic theories of intelligence accountability and governance. As Peter Gill argues, "we just do not have enough systematic knowledge about the way in which intelligence officers carry out their jobs," and as such, "there is a pressing need for research, however difficult it will be, in practice, to conduct it."[30] This book makes a modest attempt to do so, via the lens of accountability. The following section will outline the methods used in the book. It then proceeds with an analysis of the main criticisms of the existing mechanisms of accountability before going on to outline the current configuration of formal intelligence accountability in the United Kingdom.

Methodology

This book explores how intelligence accountability is understood in the U.K. context and how this links with operational practice. There have been excellent historical studies produced on the U.K. intelligence and security services and their role in government,[31] some fascinating monographs on the individual agencies and how they developed over time,[32] and also a few longer treatments on how the United Kingdom has conducted itself during the war on terror period.[33] A number of scholars have traced the emergence of legal and parliamentary accountability mechanisms.[34] Some useful work has also theorized intelligence practice and its ethical implications;[35] however, to date there has been no sustained exploration of how British intelligence and security policymakers understand accountability and how this links to institutional structures and organizational performance. Therefore, this monograph aims to fill a gap in the literature in terms of focus, while sharing the broad contemporary historical approach of other work done in this area.

The three primary intelligence-gathering agencies in the United Kingdom are: Government Communications Headquarters (GCHQ), the Secret Intelligence Service (SIS), and the Security Service (MI5). Since they are the most prominent and pervasive intelligence organizations in the country, they are the main focus of this research. GCHQ is responsible for combating cyber-threats, providing intelligence for the armed forces and government, and preventing terrorism and internet crimes such as online child abuse.[36] SIS works mostly overseas, to gather intelligence on potential threats and exploit opportunities to make contact with individuals and groups that could further British interests. Meanwhile, the Security Service operates largely (but not exclusively) at home, to combat domestic threats from terrorism, cybercrime, and espionage by hostile foreign powers.

Other key actors that make up the U.K. national intelligence machinery include the Ministry of Defence (particularly its Defence Intelligence arm), the National Security Council and Secretariat, the Joint Intelligence Organisation, the Joint Intelligence Committee (JIC), and the Office for Security and Counter-Terrorism. There are also a series of other government agencies and departments, such as the National Crime Agency, the police, the U.K. Border Agency, the Foreign and Commonwealth Office, and Her Majesty's Revenue and Customs, which produce or utilize intelligence in their activities. The latter groups will be discussed where their work links to the three primary intelligence-gathering agencies but are not the main focus of analysis since intelligence is not a core aspect of their area of responsibility. Similarly, special forces work closely with the intelligence agencies and will be referred to where relevant, but the emphasis will be on civilian agencies to provide a manageable scope for investigation.[37]

Analyzing the activities of the intelligence agencies and their accountability is difficult due to the requirement for secrecy. Only certain officials are able to speak publicly, even after retirement, and they are bound by the Official Secrets Act—as are members of the Intelligence and Security Committee (ISC) and the various commissioners who scrutinize their work. Sensitive aspects of reports are redacted; for instance, the following section appears in the 2003–04 annual report of the ISC:

> 37. We have been told that ***
> *** We are concerned that ***
> ***
> ***
> ***
> ***
> *** We will return to this matter.[38]

In this case, we learn in a later report (2004–05) that this relates to preparations for the Security Service to assume national security tasks in Northern Ireland, but in many cases the redacted material is never revealed.

Yet there is still a considerable body of scrutiny work available, through which to appraise their activities. To date (May 2019), there have been twenty-two annual reports of the ISC since its founding in 1994; sixteen ISC special reports; one annual report issued by the Investigatory Powers Commissioner's Office (IPCO); thirteen reports by their predecessor the intelligence services commissioner; ten by their forerunner, the Security Service commissioner; twenty annual reports by the interception of communications commissioner; and a special report on Section 94 of the Telecommunications Act 1984. The Investigatory Powers Tribunal has issued a series of judgments in response to complaints about the legality of the intelligence services activities, as has the High Court. There has also been a number of public inquiries, including those supervised by Lord Butler (2004) on the use of intelligence in relation to Iraq's WMD capability, Lord Hutton (2004) into the death of Dr. David Kelly (an analyst with the Defence Intelligence Staff), the Chilcot inquiry into Britain's involvement in Iraq (2009–16), as well as that of the former Intelligence Services Commissioner, Sir Peter Gibson, into the treatment of detainees (2010–12), all of which shed light on aspects of intelligence policy and operations.

The organizations themselves generally do not make public statements about their work—although as we will see, their senior staff give rare speeches and witness testimony, which are used in this book. Retired officials and government ministers have offered speeches, delivered lecture series,[39] produced news articles and comment pieces, and, occasionally, memoirs, which are all helpful sources of information on official attitudes. An important addition and correction to these texts has been the extensive media reporting of intelligence matters and reports by nongovernmental organizations and advocacy groups such as the Rendition Project, the Oxford Research Group, Amnesty International, Reprieve, Big Brother Watch, Open Rights Group, Liberty, and others. Many of the accountability issues in U.K. intelligence were first highlighted by their investigations and would never have been taken up by official scrutiny bodies if it had not been for their persistence.

In sum, although secrecy presents barriers to any external researcher on intelligence matters, a significant amount of material is in the public record, which can be utilized to formulate an understanding of how intelligence accountability works in practice. Nevertheless, due to the fragmentary nature of this evidence base, I sought to counterpoint it with semi-structured interviews with practitioners and scrutinizers. These involved posing a simple set of questions about how accountability was defined by the respondents and how they felt it operated in their experience. In questioning individuals directly, I hoped that it would be possible to probe ambiguities in the public record and uncover aspects of accountability relationships that were not articulated openly. To that end, I contacted all living former JIC chairpersons; heads of GCHQ, SIS, and MI5; ISC members; and other key individuals working in the national intelligence machinery.[40] On balance, most agreed to speak with me, but there were a number that either refused or did not respond to approaches. Of those that agreed, a number wished to be anonymous, and so to preserve this status, all interviewees were anonymized.[41]

Since my aim is to explore the meanings attached to intelligence accountability, this study adopts an interpretivist approach, looking to examine the patterns of beliefs and the interpretive efforts of participants in the national intelligence machinery—either as practitioners, scrutinizers, or commentators.[42] Informed by hermeneutics, it looks to capture the spirit of understanding in this practice, as articulated in the aforementioned official documents, as well as interviews, public speeches, media and academic commentary, and memoirs.[43] This method of reasoning is inductive and phenomenological.[44] As Ted Hopf notes: "Phenomenology implies letting the subjects speak, in this case through texts. Induction involves the recording of these identities as atheoretically as possible."[45] Rather than begin with a set of assumptions or theoretical categories, I followed Hopf's injunction to "remain ontologically open for as long as possible before imposing an analytical theoretical order, or closure, on the numerous ambiguities and differences in the texts."[46] Doing so allowed me to identify previously unspoken or under-explored aspects of accountability, such as the task-oriented and vernacular forms discussed in chapter 3. It was also particularly important to adopt an iterative approach, since interviews were conducted over a four-year period, during which a number of significant reports were issued that shed dramatic new light on intelligence practices during the post-9/11 period, from the Chilcot report in 2016 to the ISC reports on detainee abuse in 2018.

As interpretation is necessarily contingent, I acknowledge that the findings presented here may be only a partial and even ultimately inaccurate picture. There could well be disconnections between what practitioners say they do and their actual actions, between their interior motivations and those they choose to express in public forums or private interviews, and between my interpretation of texts and those of the person speaking or writing them. Attempting to draw this picture has felt at times like being a police sketch artist, relying on the memory and assertions of others to conjure up an image of something one has not seen or experienced. Nevertheless, analyzing the speeches and writings of those involved in the practice of intelligence is the best means currently available to explore intelligence accountability given the constraints of secrecy and the limits to public knowledge of what is done within this field.

The resultant analysis aims to set out the current configuration of understanding about what intelligence accountability means and how it operates in practice—while acknowledging that the interpretive environment is in a continual state of flux. The logical place to start is by delineating the overt institutional forms of accountability in the United Kingdom. The discussion then proceeds with an outline of how intelligence accountability is theorized in the academic literature, before going on to explore its interpretation in public discourse and private interviews.

Formal Intelligence Accountability in the United Kingdom

The system of intelligence accountability in place in the United Kingdom over the last two decades was heavily criticized for being both too complex and insufficiently rigorous.[47] The key actors scrutinizing intelligence activity were: the Intelligence and Security Committee (ISC); a series of commissioners, including the intelligence services commissioner, the interception of communications commissioner, and the chief surveillance commissioner; the Investigatory Powers Tribunal; and the independent reviewer of terrorism legislation. Tracing the development of these bodies over time is important, as it reveals much about public expectations around accountability compared with official attitudes—as well as allowing an understanding of how the current system came to be.

The ISC began life as a committee of parliamentarians, appointed by the prime minister under the Intelligence Services Act 1994 to oversee the work of SIS, MI5, and GCHQ. The fact that members were prime ministerial appointments was both positive and negative. On the one hand, its opinions were likely to be taken seriously as its membership had been personally approved by the prime minister. On the other hand, this selectivity risked leading to an official mind-set and lack of critical thinking, with members perhaps too ready to give agencies the benefit of the doubt. The ISC's reports contain substantial redactions and often give anodyne comments accepting the narrative offered to them by the agencies. Committee conclusions use the word "concern" to express, in an understated, British fashion, their displeasure. It is interesting to note the actions that concern them the most. Out of forty-four times that the committee used this term in their annual reports, eighteen related to policy decisions, particularly on the allocation of resources, and twelve on expenditure. Only six related to mistakes by the agencies. The most damning criticisms relate to the abandonment of the IT project SCOPE II, costing a significant amount of money, which was described as a "rather sorry saga";[48] GCHQ's poor tracking of some of its assets, including laptops, which was viewed as "unacceptable";[49] and the attempt to introduce a caveat to the agencies' sharing of information with the committee, which was admonished for being "completely unacceptable."[50]

The ISC's special reports were more rigorous. Their investigation into the murder of Lee Rigby voiced criticisms of delays in acting on intelligence and expressed surprise that MI5 "did not at those specific times place one or other of the men [i.e., the killers] under surveillance or increase their coverage of them."[51] On foreign investment in critical national infrastructure, the ISC declared itself "shocked that officials chose not to inform, let alone consult, Ministers on such an issue."[52] In its report titled *Women in the Intelligence Community*, the ISC argued with regard to GCHQ: "It is clear that any public sector organisation where 65% of employees are male, rising to 83% in the senior levels, and nearly 100% of senior staff are either white or have not declared their ethnicity, does not reflect the community it serves."[53] Yet for a long time the overall sense was of a committee that failed to scrutinize these agencies in a robust manner.[54] This appears to have been the case even when the agencies were found to have given misleading or incomplete accounts of their activities to the committee. Often these were attributed to reporting errors or narrow search terms, and the ISC would offer brief admonishments before moving on. As will be seen below, many of the most important revelations about the agencies came not from the ISC but from chance public revelations or through tenacious journalism and campaigns by activist groups.[55]

Changes were made to the ISC's workings in 2013, during the passage of the Justice and Security Act, with its remit extending to operational activity—though only retrospectively and on matters of significant national interest.[56] Curiously, the period when its powers were increased the most was also one where the committee was arguably the least rigorous in its scrutiny of the intelligence infrastructure, producing only a seventeen-page annual report with no analysis of expenditure in 2013 and no annual report for 2014–15 (although it did produce a number of special reports during this time). There was a delay of four months before the ISC was reconvened following the 2015 election, and this was extended to five months after the 2017 election, prompting criticism from the committee chair that "effective and robust oversight of the intelligence community" had been "left in a vacuum for so many months."[57]

One ISC member expressed concern that:

> the government, regardless of which party, or combination of parties, was in power, had a tendency when there was a problem to say, "We will get the ISC to look at this." And so, you then end up carrying out very specific investigations into things, which are very time-consuming, involve interviewing a lot of people, and as a result of that, I don't think sometimes that the basic job of making sure that money was spent correctly, procedures were right, and everything was being run to the book—sometimes you can't do that as well as you should do.[58]

One can imagine this kind of displacement activity serving a political purpose in allowing agencies to avoid close scrutiny of their everyday operations. Yet in doing so they would lose the benefits that come from independent assessments of their performance, in terms of correcting inefficiencies or reflecting on ways to improve effectiveness through dialogue with an informed body of commentators.

While the ISC's recent reports have offered more substantive analysis, the problem it faces has been described as whether, in the final analysis, it should be a watchdog or a cheerleader for these agencies.[59] When the

Snowden revelations were made public, it was telling that the chair of the ISC, Sir Malcolm Rifkind, leapt to the defense of the agencies on media outlets.[60] A former chair, Lord King, described this as "unfortunate," and even former practitioners saw this as an unsatisfactory response to the significance of the revelations.[61] Glees and Davies assert: "If it is the task of the agencies to 'speak truth unto power', it is the task of the ISC to 'speak truth about the agencies unto the public.' "[62] However, a former ISC member sees the duality of the ISC's role as both scrutineer and defender as less problematic:

> because we, the Committee, were within the ring of secrecy, we knew things that the media and outside didn't necessarily know, and that imposed a double duty. One duty was to criticise the agencies when they had failed in some way that might have not otherwise been apparent to the outside world. But the other was, when they were being unfairly criticised, to defend them and reassure the public that these criticisms weren't justified, and that's what Malcolm did.[63]

Mark Phythian has noted the dilemma inherent in this dual function: "what happens when the ISC finds evidence that is likely to further diminish trust in the agencies? Should it, or does it, consider how any shortcomings or criticisms should be revealed or aired so as to minimize any further erosion of public trust?"[64] Rifkind's vigorous public support for the agencies' work clearly leaned toward defender. Yet it seems strange for a scrutiny body to have, as a key part of its purpose, to represent organizations to the public while simultaneously representing the public interest in overseeing their activities. There was also criticism, even from a former senior intelligence official, when Rifkind was appointed as chair of the ISC, since he had previously been foreign secretary responsible for two of the intelligence agencies and so was viewed as unlikely to interrogate intelligence policy from first principles.[65] Since 2015, when the leadership of the committee changed to the former attorney general, Dominic Grieve, the ISC's reports have been notably more critical of the intelligence community—although this trend did begin with the Rigby report in 2013, under Rifkind.[66]

Beyond the ISC, a number of commissioners were tasked with investigating specific aspects of the intelligence agencies' work. In particular, the intelligence services commissioner was supposed to provide oversight of the exercise of Part III powers under the Regulation of Investigatory Powers Act

2000 (RIPA) as well as of the use of human sources, bulk personal data, and intrusive surveillance warrants and Section 7 actions under the Intelligence Services Act 1994.[67] The Office of Surveillance Commissioners (OSC) defined its task as "scrutinizing covert surveillance and covert human intelligence sources by public authorities in accordance with the Police Act 1997 and the Regulation of Investigatory Powers Act 2000 (RIPA)"—thus extending its remit to the police and other public bodies.[68] The Interception of Communications Commissioner's Office (IOCCO) examined the public bodies exercising authority under Part I of RIPA relating to the interception, acquisition, and disclosure of communications data.[69] In addition, the information commissioner was responsible for handling freedom of information requests that might relate to intelligence work.[70]

Overall, these commissioners had confusing and at times overlapping powers and were seen as too credulous of agency accounts of their operations. The 2014 OSC report notes matter-of-factly that "property interference authorisations were granted on 2,689 occasions; an increase of 249 on the previous year. No authorisations were quashed by Commissioners."[71] In the case of intrusive surveillance authorizations, only 2 were quashed out of 392 that year.[72] In his 2015 report, the Intelligence Services Commissioner Sir Mark Waller stated that "once again, I have not found any category C errors."[73] (Category C errors are defined as "A deliberate decision to obtain information without proper authority and with no intention to obtain proper authority."[74]) Although it is possible that agency staff were scrupulous in obtaining proper authorizations at all times, and the system of checks was rigorous, any system involving human beings will be subject to abuse at times, and so it seems strange that the commissioner was so relaxed about the absence of evidence of malpractice over a number of years.[75]

In addition to these commissioners, the Investigatory Powers Tribunal was supposed to act as an ombudsman for individuals and groups wishing to complain about surveillance conducted on them. This body originated as a result of the Regulation of Investigatory Powers Act 2000, and was formed from the merger of the Interception of Communications Tribunal with those under the Security Service Act 1989 and the Intelligence Services Act 1994. It did not have an auspicious start, with the ISC complaining that "for a significant period in 2000 the Tribunal did not have sufficient secretariat to enable it even to open the mail, let alone process and investigate complaints."[76] It was only in 2011 that tribunal members finally agreed to speak publicly with the ISC and discuss their role, despite their shared interest in the oversight of these agencies.[77] Sir David Anderson, the independent reviewer of terrorism legislation, noted that "Its profile as a robust scrutiny mechanism was not assisted by the fact that out of the 1,673 complaints determined by the end of 2013, only 10 were upheld—five of them involving members of the same family and none of them against the security and intelligence agencies."[78] It was not until the *Belhadj* judgment of April 29, 2015, that the tribunal finally found in favor of an individual against these agencies. The tribunal has been an important conduit for cases brought by campaign groups over the use of investigatory powers, but the organization itself is small and has limited resources.[79]

Since 1984, there has also been an annual review of terrorism legislation conducted by an independent reviewer. This was first put on a statutory basis through the Prevention of Terrorism Act 2005. The occupant of this role has tended to be an informed sympathetic advisor. In recent years, reviewers have produced reports that shaped government legislation—as in Anderson's *A Question of Trust* into investigatory powers.[80] They have also conducted reviews of the intelligence and security agencies after terrorist attacks—with Anderson looking into their performance after the London and Manchester incidents and his successor, Max Hill, QC, doing reports on the Westminster Bridge and London Bridge attacks. These reports were substantive but, as noted above, tended to explain away errors as systemic or a matter of bad luck.

After the 2013 Justice and Security Act reforms, most scrutiny bodies began to take a more critical approach in their investigations; yet the regime they embodied continued to be highly permissive and has been characterized as "cheerleading with caveats."[81] Recent revelations show that the Security Service failed to act over a number of years on recommendations by the Interception of Communications Commissioner's Office (IOCCO) that data collection should be authorized by someone independent of the investigation in question.[82] In other words, even when criticisms were made, they do not seem to have been acted upon. A recent judgment by the Investigatory Powers Tribunal concluded that the U.K. intelligence agencies had illegally collected communications data and confidential personal information in breach of the European Convention on Human Rights, specifically Article 8 on the right to privacy, for a period of seventeen years.[83]

To remedy the above problems, the Conservative government proposed a new Investigatory Powers Bill in 2016 based on the recommendations of three reviews into the current system: by Anderson, the ISC, and a Royal United Services Institute (RUSI) report by a panel of experts.[84] The bill proposed the creation of an Investigatory Powers Commissioner's Office (IPCO) that would merge many of the duties of the existing commissioner offices into one. This role would be supported by judicial commissioners, who would act as a "double lock," ensuring executive and judicial approval for the issuance of warrants.[85] While this does provide a check on executive power, it means that commissioners are implicated in operational decisions. In written evidence to the Public Bill committee, Dr. Tom Hickman criticized this arrangement and asserted: "The IP Bill . . . should draw a distinction between JCs whose job it is to approve or reject warrants, and inspectors who have an ex post reviewing function."[86] Otherwise, it was argued, it would be unclear who would be able to provide impartial reviews of decisionmaking.

The form of accountability envisaged under the new regime is firmly centered around legal control via judicial approval of warrants. A punitive element is also incorporated through the enhanced complaint procedures for the Investigatory Powers Tribunal. The Investigatory Powers Act received Royal Assent on November 29, 2016. The retiring commissioners submitted their final reports at the end of 2017, and so scrutiny duties passed to the Investigatory Powers Commissioner's Office (IPCO). This new body consists of sixteen judicial commissioners (including Lord Justice Sir Adrian Fulford, the investigatory powers commissioner), as well as a technical panel of experts and around fifty inspectors and support staff. It takes over the inspection and auditing duties of the three previous commissioners—IOCCO, OSC, and ISComm—and also gives prior approval to surveillance. IPCO began in August 2018 by launching a consultation at the request of the prime minister on the consolidated guidance for detaining and interviewing suspects abroad or passing intelligence related to detainees.[87] The commissioner also agreed to report on the use of young people as covert human intelligence sources (CHIS) at the request of the Home Office minister, Baroness Williams. Oversight of the intelligence and security agencies is now organized as shown in the figure that follows.

As can be seen in the figure, the system of intelligence accountability is complex, but the overall trend is of tighter controls over agencies' behav-

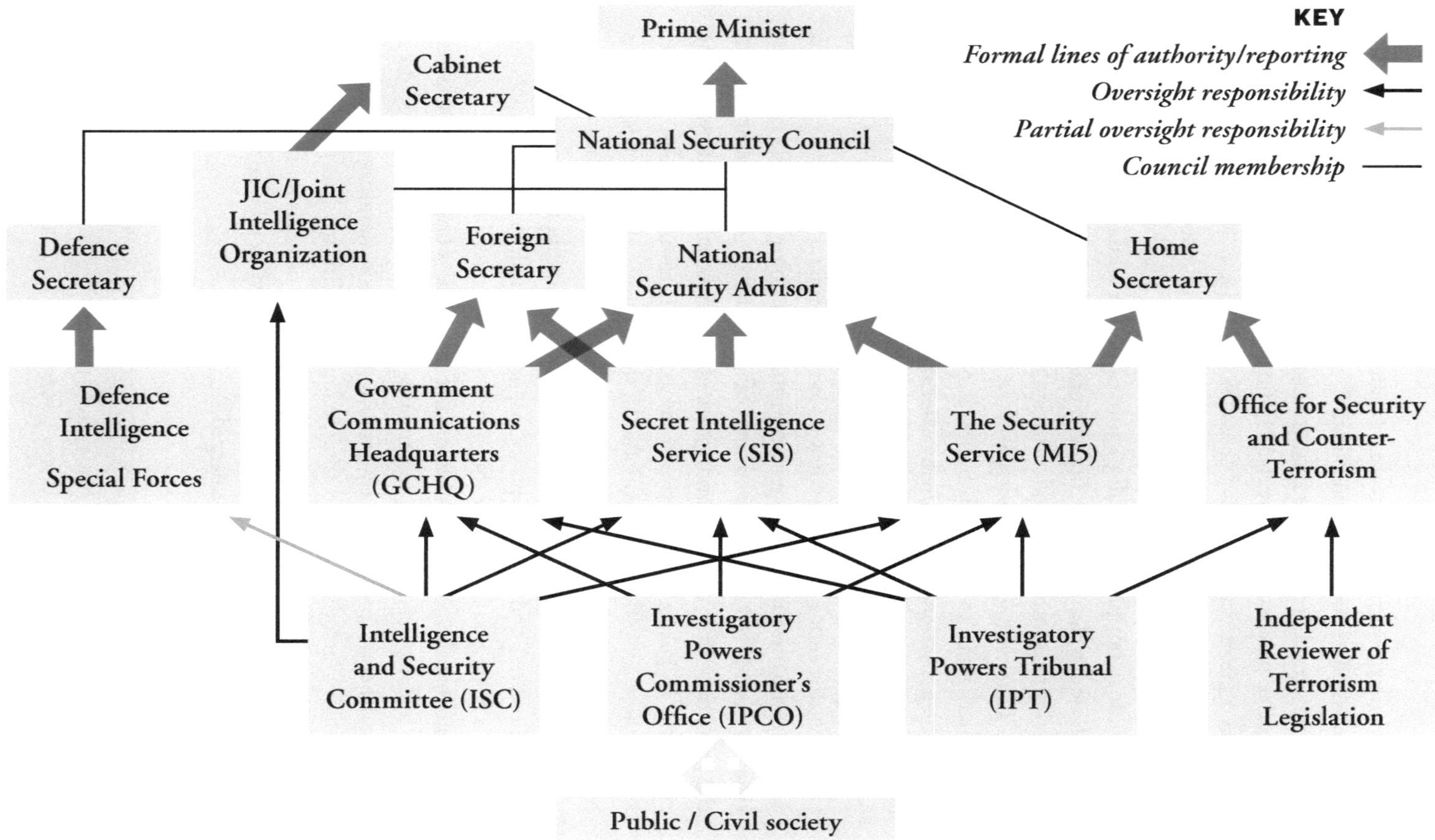
KEY
Formal lines of authority/reporting
Oversight responsibility
Partial oversight responsibility
Council membership
Prime Minister
Cabinet Secretary
National Security Council
JIC/Joint Intelligence Organization
Defence Secretary
Foreign Secretary
National Security Advisor
Home Secretary
Defence Intelligence
Special Forces
Government Communications Headquarters (GCHQ)
Secret Intelligence Service (SIS)
The Security Service (MI5)
Office for Security and Counter-Terrorism
Intelligence and Security Committee (ISC)
Investigatory Powers Commissioner's Office (IPCO)
Investigatory Powers Tribunal (IPT)
Independent Reviewer of Terrorism Legislation
Public / Civil society

ior, particularly with regard to legal frameworks. The previous patchwork of commissioners has been consolidated, and the ISC has been given enhanced powers. There is now a greater willingness on the ISC's part to criticize negative practices and perceived failings in the intelligence machinery, as well as a greater openness in discussion of intelligence practice thanks to a number of reviews and inquiries. However, as will be seen in the following chapters, this tendency to view accountability as about control and public criticism does not present a full picture of how it actually operates in this sphere. If one explores how intelligence practitioners perceive the concept of accountability, control and condemnation are only part of a wider and more complex system of account-giving and -receiving across government. What keeps intelligence professionals honest is not just ministerial oversight, the threat of legal action, or scrutiny by external bodies, but also organizational culture and self-identity. Despite the constraints of secrecy, officials share ideas, conduct challenge exercises, submit themselves to peer review, and engage with a series of stakeholders—from academia, civil society, and industry to organizations and agencies from other countries. The desire for efficiency is derived not just from lines of authority in government but also the tasks they seek to fulfill and, particularly, the challenge presented by opponents in hostile states, terrorist networks, or criminal gangs. In other words, there are official and nonofficial, formal and informal mechanisms of accountability operating simultaneously across the intelligence community in the United Kingdom. What follows is an attempt to uncover these under-theorized and under-explored aspects of intelligence accountability to offer a fuller picture of how they inform intelligence practice.

To summarize, the central dilemma of this book is how intelligence and security agencies can be held accountable when much of what they do is secret and hence inscrutable. By exploring the understanding of accountability among practitioners and commentators, it aims to identify what processes shape the ethical sensibilities of intelligence officials and, ultimately, suggest ways that accountability could be improved to minimize the errors and ethical failings that have emerged.

ONE

Accountability and Intelligence

This chapter explores what is meant by accountability in the intelligence realm and considers why holding intelligence practitioners to account is seen as particularly challenging. Is there something inherent to the practice that makes accountability so difficult? Or is it more the way intelligence is framed and how secrecy is used to close off discussion and direct criticisms toward certain specific areas rather than others? To consider how intelligence and accountability interrelate, this chapter will address some basic questions, such as: what does accountability mean in this sphere? Why is it important? Who should practice it? What is it supposed to achieve? The focus of this discussion will be the secondary literature from "external" commentators. Analyzing these interpretations will provide a useful context and framework for the later chapters exploring the understandings of accountability in a national and international context, among overseers, commentators, and practitioners.

What Does Accountability Mean in an Intelligence Context?

Accountability can be defined in a number of ways. In the public policy literature, it is variously described as the "exchange of reasons for conduct,"[1] the "enforcement of standards and the fulfilment of obligations,"[2] "responsiveness,"[3] and "providing answers for your behavior."[4] Although linked, each of these indicates a different interpretation of what this term connotes—from sharing knowledge to enforcing norms, allocating responsibility or rationalizing and justifying action. A common thread across most definitions is the idea of accountability as a process whereby one actor provides an account of themselves and their behavior to another individual or group. A predefined role and set of responsibilities for the account giver are usually implied, along with parameters of appropriate behavior. The receiver is there to judge how far they have fulfilled their duties, in a way commensurate with the role and its associated norms. (The account receiver could be internal or external to the organization, depending on the circumstances.)

Accountability is therefore broadly comprised of two components: "rendering account," which is the provision of information, and "holding to account," whereby a judgment is made about the appropriateness of behavior, based on this and other information.[5] Furthermore, as noted in the introduction, the actions of the intelligence and security agencies are usually appraised according to their perceived efficiency, effectiveness, and ethics.[6] These three categories are explored in more depth later in this chapter.

In practical terms, rendering an account involves giving a narrative of what actions were taken, by whom, when, and why. In order for it to be intelligible to a third party, this narrative requires an explanation of the context to these actions, setting them within a particular time and space. A rich account could therefore entail sharing a significant amount of information about what took place and why. For this reason, accountability is problematic for intelligence agencies since secrecy and the restriction of information to as few people as possible has traditionally been central to their practice.[7] Yet accountability can take place within as well as outside an organization, and so account-giving is not precluded in the intelligence realm, provided the receiver is within the "ring of secrecy."

The accountability literature tends to draw a distinction between public accountability—between organizations and external bodies—and bureaucratic accountability, which is internal to an organization.[8] Broadly, public accountability takes legal and political forms and is about public control and democratic participation; meanwhile, internal accountability is focused on technical performance and the upholding of professional standards.[9] However, the division is not straightforward in practice since failures in performance or professional norms have legal and political consequences and public scrutiny is supposed to check for malfeasance and inefficiency.[10] Nevertheless, discussion of accountability in the intelligence realm overwhelmingly focuses on external public accountability at the expense of internal aspects.

In the intelligence field, the label "oversight" is often applied to describe forms of public accountability via legislative scrutiny bodies, inspectors general, or commissioners. The term connotes a detached, external observer providing a general level of scrutiny in a limited fashion. It is important to note that this type of public accountability is elite-focused: accountability is what happens when the heads of intelligence agencies provide a narrative of their behavior to, and answer questions from, external scrutiny bodies or informed individuals in the legislature, judiciary, or executive. Internal bureaucratic accountability, whereby officials are accountable to their line managers and so on up the chain to the head of the organization, is rarely mentioned. Nor is there much suggestion that public bodies should be able to seek accounts from lower-level officials about the workings of the intelligence agencies. Depending on the issue, the emphasis is on either the head or the minister providing an account to external interested parties.

This is a broad feature of much civil service accountability in the United Kingdom, but it is taken to the extreme in the case of the intelligence services. It is worth recalling that other forms of accountability are possible. For example, under a system of collective accountability, any member of the organization can be called to account for the actions of the group.[11] Alternatively, in a system of individual accountability, individuals at any level in the bureaucracy can be questioned about their actions and their responsibility for collective outcomes.[12] Focusing accountability on a senior figure serves political purposes. It reduces the scope for questions about operational performance, instead lending itself to general queries of policy over which the head of an organization would have daily control. It also restricts knowledge flows to a single stovepipe that can shape the information shared with others. Moreover, it preserves the impression of the intelligence machinery as a closed environment beyond public scrutiny. The ISC has tried unsuccessfully to challenge this understanding and question mid- and lower-level officials about the United Kingdom's conduct during the war on terror period. The government's refusal to allow this led the ISC to conclude that they could not provide a full and rigorous scrutiny of intelligence policy and practice.[13]

In oversight forums, the agency head will normally defend their budget, explain their implementation of policy, deflect criticism, and jockey for more powers, but the efficiency of their organization (and particularly their effectiveness) is a mystery. While this preserves the secrecy of the intelligence environment, it reinforces a sense of distance between the agencies and the society they are protecting. The result is a limited dialogue, which inhibits the free exchange of ideas and information that might test orthodoxies and propose new ways of understanding and doing intelligence work. Nor is it straightforward to see such accountability gaps being filled by the executive. Ministers, who are supposed to oversee agency activities on behalf of the general public, are unlikely to challenge prevailing assumptions since they set the policy and so are implicated in operational decisions.[14]

Elite accountability carries with it some advantages that could serve the public good. For instance, it offers an opportunity for senior intelligence managers to reflect on their own policy assumptions and test them against informed commentators—within narrow parameters. The requirement to construct a narrative that rationalizes, explains, and justifies their existence and behavior to others cannot help but compel reflection—even if the narrative they present is not necessarily a true reflection of their self-identity or a full picture of their activities. Separating those who are undertaking intelligence activities from those who are meant to judge their rightness could also be useful—allowing clear lines of responsibility and blame, with the caveat that in doing so it may reinforce an "us and them" mentality, obscuring the fact that the agencies and the scrutiny bodies are all supposed to be acting in the wider public interest.[15]

Nevertheless, if elite accountability inhibits proper analysis of the performance and internal norms of intelligence organizations, this is problematic, as it means much of their daily activity is beyond scrutiny. A number of other factors also limit the range of "account-giving" in the intelligence context and mean that the concept is often understood in narrow ways. These include secrecy, limited organizational knowledge, legal controls, the separation of the domestic and foreign spheres, and the tendency to focus on retrospective punishment rather than learning.[16] These will be analyzed in turn before considering why accountability is important, who should conduct it, and what it is meant to achieve.

Limitations on Intelligence Accountability

Secrecy presents a problem for accountability because it seems to act in tension with the aims of the latter. Secrecy is about restricting knowledge flows and maintaining an informational advantage over rivals, whereas giving an account—especially if it is public—inevitably means sharing information and thereby reducing the mystique of an organization and its working practices. In some senses, changes to intelligence practice in recent years have made accountability and secrecy more compatible. Western governments have widened the ring of secrecy to enable a much greater range of agencies and officials to access intelligence since 9/11, to the extent that Richard Aldrich and Christopher Moran estimate "in the United States, over 5 million people enjoy security clearances."[17] In an effort to avoid the "silo thinking" that supposedly prevented connections being made that might have stopped the 9/11 terrorist attacks from happening,[18] there is now a much denser matrix of cooperation and dialogue between agencies. Similarly, in the United Kingdom, Alex Younger, the chief of SIS, has argued: "the key point that sets us apart as an intelligence community is our ability to work together. We have powerful but distinct capabilities. We are able to succeed through our ability to fuse them together, to become far more than the sum of our parts."[19] The corollary of this is that organizations have far more scope to give accounts of their behavior and open up their actions to scrutiny by peers and colleagues than in the past.

Yet the unintended effects of these policies have contributed to what Aldrich and Richterova term a "crisis of secrecy," pitting accountability and secrecy against one another once again.[20] The sheer number of people privy to secret intelligence has resulted in "ambient accountability," whereby wrongdoing is more easily exposed and "Disgruntled officials can now harvest and release entire archives of secret material with a pen drive."[21] Technology has thereby enabled more secrets to be collected but at the same time made them less secure as they are more easily shared. In response, governments are now deploying technology to identify in advance who might be "pre-leakers"—those liable to be future whistleblowers.[22] Yet in doing so they may be stigmatizing morally conscientious workers whose removal would narrow the scope for ethical challenge and debate within the organization. In short, secrecy and accountability remain in tension, and secrecy and technology may in the future combine to reduce accountability.

Secrecy does not only make account-giving and receiving difficult, but also makes it harder to evaluate the accuracy of those accounts. This applies both to the specific information relayed and the wider institutional context. Lack of organizational knowledge and information is an important and linked factor preventing external bodies from gaining a detailed picture of what really goes on within the intelligence services. In the U.K. context, the various commissioners expressed a desire in their reports to understand the organizational culture of the intelligence agencies and get a sense of their bureaucratic norms. However, these efforts were very impressionistic. The Intelligence and Security Committee (ISC) is said to have tried to focus more on effectiveness rather than just democratic control and propriety.[23] Yet this has been a slow process, partly due to its external institutional position: for all the selectivity of its membership and reporting, it is made up of parliamentarians—not current or former intelligence officials. Coupled with its limited resources and powers (albeit bolstered by reforms in 2013), and opportunity to talk only to agency heads, it has struggled to dig deeper into operational performance. When the ISC does comment on matters such as resources, IT systems, and buildings, this has been dismissed as little more than acting as "management consultants for the government" rather than being a rigorous source of critique on intelligence practices.[24] The U.K. intelligence machinery has been more open since it was put on a statutory basis, but practitioners and scrutineers are bound by the Official Secrets Act, and the numbers of people employed, even with its expansion, is quite small, totaling 17,331 in the main agencies, according to the most recent figures.[25] Therefore, few commentators have actually worked with or for these organizations, and those that have are not able to speak freely about how official narratives compare with their experiences.

The limitations of the ISC's membership are exacerbated by the technological advances affecting intelligence work. Data collection software and protocols require considerable technical knowledge to understand. Although ISC members have tended to have experience in the broad security field, as junior foreign or defense ministers, or academics, they are unlikely to have the technical background to allow a detailed evaluation of the implications of how agencies use technology in intelligence work—something exposed during the Snowden revelations.[26]

Legal mechanisms of accountability provide a higher level of control; however, in the case of the intelligence services this is qualified by the demands of national security. In the United Kingdom, the agencies operate on a statutory legal basis—with the Secret Intelligence Service governed by the Intelligence Services Act 1994 and the Security Service by the Security Service Act 1989. There are also important legal means of redress against these agencies, such as the European Convention on Human Rights and the domestic Human Rights Act 1998. Yet judges have been reluctant to rule against governmental policy made on national security grounds. In the past they have questioned the legality of some counterterrorism measures such as control orders (whereby individuals had restrictions placed on their movement and communications), but the decision to derogate from Article 5(1) of the European Convention relating to the right to liberty of terrorist suspects (on the Article 15 basis that the United Kingdom faced a "Public Emergency which Threatens the Life of the Nation") was described by a senior judge as "a preeminently political judgment" and so outside their expertise.[27] Similarly, the policy of bulk data capture—where agencies collected communications data from the entire U.K. population of users—has not been criticized by courts in principle, but rather in terms of practice.[28]

The distinction between judicial and executive control is challenged by the reforms of the Investigatory Powers Act 2016. By introducing judicial commissioners, who must make a judgment about the necessity and proportionality of warrant requests to search communications data or conduct surveillance, the act blurs the lines between judicial and executive aspects of accountability. The risk of this change is that moral and political elements of decisionmaking may be downplayed in favor of technical discussions of whether activities comply with the letter of the law.[29] Although evaluating necessity and proportionality would have to include some consideration of these elements, this would be done with reference to legislation and could marginalize wider public interest concerns. Furthermore, it is notable that the advisory notice explaining the commissioners' approach to approving warrants states: "On certain issues, such as, for example, what counts as legitimate ways to achieve foreign policy or national security priorities, the judicial commissioners' reviewing role will be necessarily limited and the judicial commissioners will afford a very wide margin of judgment to the secretary of state in determining such matters."[30] Overall, putting the secret agencies on a statutory basis and giving the judiciary a greater role in determining intelligence activity has increased the breadth and depth of account-giving. In that sense, accountability has been strengthened. Yet this operates within defined parameters and downplays important political and ethical questions about what is right and appropriate in favor of what is legal.

Another factor delimiting accountability in the intelligence context is a tendency to separate the domestic and foreign spheres. Activities within the former are subject to greater controls, while the latter can often enjoy remarkable freedom from scrutiny and auditing. For example, intrusive surveillance operations in the United Kingdom by British intelligence and security personnel require a ministerial warrant, yet abroad they are grouped as class authorizations under the Intelligence Services Act 1994. The Intelligence and Security Committee has noted that "agencies do not all keep detailed records of operational activity conducted under class authorizations."[31] As such, close scrutiny of the appropriateness of individual cases abroad is not possible. Similarly, in the United States the political controversy over Edward Snowden's revelations about bulk data collection centered on the idea that in spying on the communications of foreign individuals, the U.S. government was collecting the private messages of U.S. citizens as well.[32] This was seen as contrary to the Foreign Intelligence Surveillance Act of 1978, which required a warrant for surveillance on U.S. citizens. In other words, different standards and expectations of accountability apply, depending on where the activity is taking place and against whom.[33]

The final factor constraining intelligence accountability is the fact that it is almost entirely retrospective. The combination of a closed, secret system, little attention to internal standards and behavior, and a focus of scrutiny on the domestic realm means that intelligence accountability has tended to be centered on "firefighting"—that is, responding to flagrant breaches of standards or intelligence failures that emerge from either whistleblowers, policy errors, or surprise attacks.[34] Day-to-day "police patrolling" activities by scrutiny bodies like the U.K. Intelligence and Security Committee have been seen as flawed thanks to misleading accounts provided by officials (see chapter 2)—even when this body was made up of prime ministerial appointees and its reports could be heavily redacted to avoid compromising operations. Levels of "responsiveness" and interest in "providing answers" that are accurate tend to depend on wider public engagement in the media or via court processes—what Richard Aldrich terms "regulation by revelation."[35]

Such scrutiny is likely to be more confrontational and provoke defensive responses. It is also arguably damaging to the spirit of accountability overall, as it conflates account-giving with punishment. (In the United Kingdom, punishment does not usually take the form of dismissal or criminal prosecution but rather negative publicity, reputational damage, and political embarrassment—what Mark Bovens has labeled "face consequences.")[36] While the capacity to punish is a factor in any effective system of accountability, there has to be more to giving accounts than anticipating public censure—otherwise, the tendency will always be to avoid presenting a full narrative that acknowledges errors and allows genuine learning. As Glenn Hastedt notes, during and immediately after crisis situations, "the learning capacity of leaders and organizations is low" and so focusing accountability on events like these means that it is likely to be ineffective at improving future behavior.[37] Furthermore, since this form of accountability is retrospective, it is rather too easy for agencies to say that lessons have been learned, personnel have moved on, and that particular mistakes could not be repeated. It is also important to note that as the current oversight system in the United Kingdom does not allow whistleblowers to provide accounts to external bodies, with the possible exception of the ISC, individuals outside the agencies can only respond to concerns once they have become public via the media.

The introduction of judicial commissioners approving warrants (for domestic surveillance) does, for the first time, provide an element of real-time accountability, since this is supposed to be undertaken prior to the warrant being executed. If a warrant is required as a matter of urgency, and there is not time to gain judicial assent, the agency must report this to a judicial commissioner, who has to make a judgment within three working days as to its appropriateness and can cancel the warrant and order the destruction of material obtained.[38] Most processes of account-giving are retrospective as a matter of course, however. As noted above, the ISC explicitly excludes ongoing operations from its scrutiny.

In summary, accountability in the U.K. intelligence realm is restricted, elite-focused, largely retrospective, punitive (in terms of reputational damage), focuses on policy more than practice, and applies different standards of scrutiny depending on whether the activity is perceived as within the domestic or foreign spheres. This approach is driven by the imperative of secrecy and designed to minimize disruption to the work of the intelligence agencies. It assumes a high level of integrity on the part of officials and provides minimal oversight from the judiciary (except when it comes to warrants), legislature, or wider public. While executive approval is required for legally or politically sensitive operations, the extent to which this constitutes accountability in terms of oversight is clouded by the fact that ministers set policy. An example of confusion in this regard is apparent in the former British Foreign Secretary Jack Straw's attempts to deny knowledge of rendition operations allegedly facilitated by MI6 during his tenure. News reports suggested that officials paid him a visit and reminded him that he had signed off on these actions and so shared responsibility.[39]

Why Is Accountability Important?

The most obvious reason for concern over accountability is that organizations that are closed to external scrutiny are more open to abuse.[40] As Michael Andregg puts it: "Power tends to corrupt even the most open system; secret power systems and the people in them are especially vulnerable to this. Hubris corrupts all professions."[41] This is often highlighted as a danger to society, but it is also important for the intelligence organizations themselves. Ineffective accountability allows individuals the freedom to subvert organizational norms and standards.[42] This can manifest itself in a number of ways. At the collective level, officials may lose sight of the wider public good and seek to advance organizational goals—even where they conflict with the public interest. Tim Weiner has suggested that CIA officials during the Cold War "were prepared to lie to the president to protect the agency's image."[43] Alternatively, they might breach organizational norms where they perceive them to be an obstacle to wider public safety. The same author cites the CIA's deputy director of plans, Richard J. Bissell, as saying: "Many of us who joined the CIA did not feel bound in the actions we took as staff members to observe all the ethical rules."[44] Ian Cobain has alleged that the U.K. intelligence and security agencies continued to use the "five techniques" to interrogate Northern Irish detainees suspected of terrorism despite explicit prime ministerial orders to suspend the practice.[45] In some of these instances, the officials might not be acting in bad faith as such, but rather interpreting their priorities according to their own perception of operational requirements, in ways that may be unethical but are unchecked in the accountability vacuum.[46]

A separate set of problems comes from those who are motivated by individual rather than collective goals. Favoritism, bullying, paranoia, a focus on pet projects rather than collectively important tasks, personal aggrandizement via empire-building, and rent-seeking can all flourish in bureaucracies without external scrutiny.[47] In addition, individual ideological motivations can subvert collective norms—as in the case of double agents, coup plotters, or obsessive mole-hunters.[48] Peter Wright's role in MI5 as a counter-espionage operator combines all three elements, and Stella Rimington's account of the disruptive effect of this individual on the Security Service's performance is illustrative:

> by the time I knew him he was quite clearly a man with an obsession and was regarded . . . as quite mad and certainly dangerous. . . . He was self-important, he had an over-developed imagination and an obsessive personality which had turned to paranoia. And above all he was lazy. . . . It was hard to explain why he was allowed to stay for so long . . . He used to wander around, finding out what everyone was doing, taking cases off people, going off and doing interviews which he never wrote up, and then moving on to something else, while refusing to release files for others to work on.[49]

Having exhibited excessive levels of trust in officials and low accountability prior to the discovery of the Cambridge spy ring, the U.K. intelligence services would move to becoming "very inward-looking and to be extremely anxious about whether they had got traitors within their organization."[50] Mistrust permeated the organizations with consequent effects on efficiency, staff morale, and cohesion. One former SIS officer noted "a pervasive lack of institutional self-confidence" for decades afterward, which was "quite something when you consider how far back Philby actually was."[51] The risk in responding to failures of accountability is that it might lead to "accountability ping-pong," with formerly lax oversight becoming far more restrictive and burdensome before eventually having to be loosened again, something often seen as a feature of the intelligence field.[52]

Concerns that bureaucracies are acting beyond their powers or avoiding scrutiny are common, in one form or another, in many organizational contexts, but are particularly problematic in the intelligence realm because of the nature of that practice. Intelligence officials engaged in espionage are breaking the law—even if it is usually the law of a foreign state. Agents have to intentionally deceive others, at times spreading misinformation, falsely representing themselves, and offering commitments they may not be able to fulfill. Eliciting information via interrogation, coercion, or exploitation will routinely entail the manipulation of an individual to serve a purpose that will go against that individual's interest. Such methods are not the entirety of intelligence practice, but they are an important component. Even intelligence fields such as signals intelligence (SIGINT), which do not involve direct person-to-person contact, entail observing individuals without their knowledge and prying into their personal lives in ways that are deeply intrusive and would be seen as voyeurism in other contexts. As a result, a significant amount of the work of these agencies involves behavior that is contrary to normal ethical codes.[53] The pressures of such work on the moral sensibilities of practitioners are considerable. Accountability has the capacity to enable a twofold process of keeping individuals in these agencies honest as well as reassuring them that their behavior is in accordance with the public good.

Academic commentators have tended to portray the U.K. national intelligence machinery as historically cautious and wary of overreaching its power or undermining democratic processes domestically.[54] David Cameron complains in his memoirs that SIS, along with the military, was "a huge source of frustration" on Syria in their reluctance to propose options for covert action.[55] Richard Aldrich and Rory Cormac suggest that SIS refused to cooperate with mooted prime ministerial plans to assassinate foreign leaders on at least two occasions in the postwar period.[56] Meanwhile, Harold Wilson's cabinet secretary in the 1960s, Burke Trend, is said to have "gasped in horror at the thought of probing the private lives of MPs" when urged to do so by the paymaster general, George Wigg.[57] Clearly, the record is mixed, and there were instances of overbearing behavior, but it is interesting that SIS and the Security Service expressed concern at the "confusion over lines of ministerial accountability" that Wigg's muckraking activities for Wilson had wrought.[58] Given the lack of oversight in this period, there had to be an element of self-restraint on their part; otherwise their presence in public life would surely have been much more intrusive.

From a practical perspective, even if these agencies can somehow preserve their virtue without external pressure, they will struggle hard not to become sclerotic or irrelevant. Organizations that avoid rigorous external or internal review risk atrophy.[59] Therefore, it is in the agencies' own interest to have their assumptions challenged and their behavior scrutinized so that they can root out bad policy, receive new and innovative ideas, and be confident they are operating effectively.[60] The dangers of a lack of rigor in intelligence analysis were brought sharply home by the Chilcot report into the United Kingdom's decision to participate in the invasion of Iraq in 2003. In addition to outlining the numerous errors in the assessment of Iraq's capabilities, the inquiry noted that "At no stage was the proposition that Iraq might no longer have chemical, biological, or nuclear weapons or programmes identified and examined by either the JIC [Joint Intelligence Committee] or the policy community."[61] Poor scrutiny by policymakers had combined with official myopia to entrench the assumption that Iraq possessed WMD, even as the evidence from inspections began to suggest otherwise.[62]

To overcome closed-mindedness in bureaucracies, Rascoff advocates a "risk management" approach to intelligence governance involving greater transparency and "rationality review" via cost-benefit analyses. Yet transparency presents self-evident problems for secret organizations.[63] Also, for all the popularity of a risk-management approach in current public policy thinking, it can be problematic. Risk is not an objective category—in fact, done properly, risk analysis acknowledges its subjective nature and is clear about the contingent nature of its assumptions.[64] Employing terms like "rationality review" conveys a sense of logical and dispassionate judgment. When it is coupled with the notion of a "cost-benefit analysis," we are presented with a depoliticized, mechanistic process when the reality is far more complex and highly political. Nevertheless, Rascoff's proposals are important if only because they begin to break down the wall between organizational performance and external scrutiny bodies, opening up a space for internal account-giving to be incorporated into the overall system of accountability.

In short, contrary to much of the emphasis in academic and policy circles on accountability as important for democratic control, the above discussion has highlighted some of the organizational and operational benefits that it can provide. Internal account-giving—rendering internal accounts—can reinforce organizational norms, allow reflection on performance and learning for the future, highlight malpractice, and promote innovation. To ignore or downplay these processes and only focus on external mechanisms of account-giving—holding to account—is to present an incomplete picture of intelligence accountability.

Who Should Hold Intelligence Agencies to Account?

Advocating transparency and reviews begs the question of who would be able to supply such an appraisal. Current practitioners may be too close to the agencies to give objective commentary; former practitioners or retirees might be out of touch with modern methods, tools, and norms; peer reviewers from foreign agencies would not share the cultural awareness of why things are done the way they are; meanwhile, parliamentarians may not have the technical expertise to understand and critique the use of technology.[65] Anyone given access to sensitive material would have to undergo a substantial vetting process that itself might contain the seeds of unconscious bias toward those of a sympathetic mind-set.

In other words, intelligence accountability forums face a "legitimacy-accountability paradox." There is a trade-off, whereby those most able to judge the effectiveness of these organizations (through their knowledge and experience) are also those least likely to be seen as legitimate scrutinizers by third parties, because of their status as "insiders." Conversely, those more obviously independent and resistant to in-group pressures and socialization within government, such as members of nongovernmental organizations, the media, and citizen groups, are also most likely to be perceived by the agencies as either ill-informed, partisan, or potential security threats, and so are unlikely to be offered fulsome and accurate accounts of agency activities.[66] Having informed experts with prior experience scrutinize the agencies can make their conclusions more authoritative, even if activist groups might question their independence. As Jonathan Simon stated in relation to investigatory commissions: "The fact that typical commission members have already given distinguished government service of some sort is less a guarantee of independence . . . than an assurance that the speaker is the sort of person whose criticism is to be taken seriously."[67]

Yet the risk in asking former grandees to hold intelligence agencies accountable is that they will be unable or unwilling to question intelligence activities from first principles and do the necessary digging to expose malpractice. Loch Johnson has pointed out that in the United States "None of the major intelligence abuses that came to light during the 1960s and 1970s were uncovered by institutions of accountability inside the executive branch, but rather by media and congressional investigators."[68] The same applies to the United Kingdom.[69] As noted above, it was activist groups, academics, and the media who first brought to public attention the United Kingdom's involvement in rendition and policies on bulk data capture.

In the absence of effective scrutiny, it is perhaps surprising that abuses of power are not more common. Scholars have explained this as a result of the continual and important constraining effects of internal organizational norms that serve to check the abuse of power and hold personnel to account via the judgment of their peers.[70] Here, logics of appropriateness govern behavior and shape the accounts offered.[71] Yet it is just such forms of account-giving that are largely excluded from current accountability reforms and much academic commentary. If it really is these mechanisms that are most important to curtailing widespread abuse, then they deserve far more attention than they presently receive. Opening them up to scrutiny is vital, because maintaining a closed culture with very rigid norms is only likely to make accountability more difficult in the long run. The tendency will be for officials to close ranks to enforce group loyalty. Thus, the abuse of power may be more widespread than we realize, but group cohesion is preventing such information from coming to light.

Given these concerns, commentators from outside the intelligence community tend to favor more rigorous scrutiny by external bodies; however, that may be due to there being different "epistemic communities" at play. Academics see wider dissemination of knowledge as more conducive to collective learning and discovery. But in the realm of national security, such a move carries risks. Most obviously, there is the potential for security breaches as the circle of those privy to secret information widens to individuals who have not been vetted as systematically, may not be as adept at maintaining security protocols, or who cannot be sanctioned in the same way as an official with a career and a pension. If the individual scrutinizer is part of the legislature, there is a serious risk of political grandstanding.[72] This can be aimed at privileging a rival organization, furthering their own career profile, or, often linked, at using accountability mechanisms to attack the executive. The roving inquiry into Hillary Clinton's role in the death of the U.S. ambassador to Libya in 2012 carried strong implications of such behavior.[73]

These sorts of manipulations of accountability generally corrode public trust without benefiting the public good, because they are designed to further a sectional or individual interest rather than improve performance. Their focus tends to be more on punishment and humiliation of individuals than organizational learning and adaptation. Even when external observers are acting in good faith and with diligence, their lack of experience in the practices they are scrutinizing can create difficulties due to a lack of awareness of what is normal and what would be a breach of etiquette—as well as how operational demands may impinge on effectiveness. An example in the U.K. context was Lord Hutton's failure, in his inquiry in 2004, to appreciate just how unusual it was for the prime minister's communication staff to be handling intelligence material, working closely with the Joint Intelligence Committee in producing reports, and having a say in their presentation to the public.[74]

This leads us to consider the role of the media in soliciting information from the intelligence machinery and holding it to account. Claudia Hillebrand notes three ways in which the news media contribute to oversight of the agencies and can thereby link to accountability. First, they operate as an "information transmitter," bringing to light information on intelligence activity to the wider public.[75] The general public knows far more about what is done in their name thanks to coverage of intelligence stories, the reporting of leaks, and recording of criminal cases. Second, they can operate as a "substitute watchdog,"[76] uncovering evidence of possible wrongdoing and questioning the executive when formal oversight bodies fail to do so. In addition, they play a legitimizing role for the intelligence services, reporting their successes and offering them a means to communicate with the general populace.[77]

The media's role in holding governments to account is problematic, however. In the United Kingdom, scrutiny has historically been hampered by the blanket refusal by agencies and ministers to respond to media queries on intelligence. Thus, in response to a story in 2014 that the government was harvesting private information on users of the smartphone app Angry Birds, as well as Facebook and YouTube, GCHQ stated: "It is a longstanding policy that we do not comment on intelligence matters."[78] While the official "no comment" policy is a useful way for the agencies to avoid awkward questions, it also means that the agencies have not historically been able to refute erroneous reporting or laud their successes publicly—though plenty of informal tip-offs and briefings have been proffered to selected journalists.[79] Thus, the media's ability to act as an information transmitter is limited. The existence of the "D notice" system also constrains how much intelligence information the media communicates to the public.[80] Now termed DSMA (Defense and Security Media Advisory) notices, these are a mechanism by which newspapers clear certain stories with the intelligence and security agencies before publication to ensure they do not risk national security or public safety. Some newspapers have avoided using the system at times, to ensure that sensitive stories were not blocked, as when the *Observer* published a story on United Kingdom spying on the United Nations in 2004 and the *Guardian* published its first leaks from Edward Snowden.[81] But it is generally upheld and so acts as a barrier to full public disclosure of intelligence stories.

The U.K. media's capacity to act as a substitute watchdog has been significantly eroded in recent years due to the nature of the business environment it inhabits. Traditional print media are facing severe budgetary constraints as a result of declining readership and advertising revenue—in part, thanks to the advent of online and new social media. That means that lengthy news investigations into intelligence matters are increasingly burdensome. The kinds of stories that will "make" are likely to have an emphasis on novelty and contain a strong element of human interest. Thus, long-running issues struggle to compete for public attention and gradual changes over time—particularly structural or systemic ones—are unlikely to be reported.

While there are still some newspapers of record that can be consulted by the public, there is a massive array of internet news traffic, which can drown out more nuanced narratives. Important matters of context and analysis are often lost. In addition, there are actors who use these forums for ideological purposes. Groups such as Wikileaks are regularly criticized for publishing secret information without due concern for the safety of individuals listed in their data dumps.[82] The exposure of the full range of communications between governments—and of the actions of soldiers, diplomats, and civil servants acting on their behalf—is often defended as giving the public the chance to be truly informed, but it also arguably has the effect of subverting government itself. If governments are unable to have private conversations, the result would be severe poverty of rigorous policy discussion and the curtailment of a huge amount of legitimate diplomatic activity. It would also attack the very notion of secret intelligence, since nothing could be secret and, as everyone is privy to the knowledge, it no longer carries the informational advantage associated with "intelligence."

It is important to note that these leaks tend to have an unduly negative effect on advanced democratic governments, whose systems are more open to scrutiny compared to authoritarian and/or less developed states (although Wikileaks' revelations about the Tunisian president Ben Ali's family business concerns were credited with contributing to the toppling of the regime and the advent of the Arab Spring).[83] Nevertheless, while their primary impact seems to be to foster a general distrust of intelligence, they do regularly provoke traditional accountability forums in Parliament and Whitehall into requesting accounts from agencies about their activities, if only to refute allegations.

More unequivocally negative are the concerted efforts by states such as Russia to exploit the proliferation of media outlets in the West and promote disinformation.[84] In a speech he made in 2018, the director general of the

Security Service, Andrew Parker, described the problems hostile state activity in the online realm poses for the agencies and their efforts to inform the public:

> Age-old attempts at covert influence and propaganda have been supercharged in online disinformation, which can be churned out at massive scale and little cost. The aim is to sow doubt by flat denials of the truth, to dilute truth with falsehood, divert attention to fake stories, and do all they can to divide alliances. Barefaced lying seems to be the default mode, coupled with ridicule of critics.[85]

Parker lumps in media manipulation and social media disinformation with espionage and military force as part of a set of "hybrid threats" to the United Kingdom from Russia, in particular. Combined with the ideological agenda of anti-secrecy groups like Wikileaks, they represent a serious challenge to the ability of new forms of media to foster a constructive environment for account-giving. Of course, it is also important to note that the U.K. government exploited media interest in intelligence to justify intervention in Iraq in 2003—leading to misleading reports about national security threats. In doing so, it provoked greater skepticism about the veracity of intelligence reporting and the good faith of intelligence officials, creating a climate where government statements and media reporting could be challenged by, and given equal weight to, nonexpert opinion, especially in online forums. The U.K. government is therefore partly responsible for the decline in trust that followed.

When it comes to commentary on intelligence accountability, few authors consider the idea that the general public might play a role in holding intelligence and security services to account. The heads of the intelligence and security agencies gave evidence in public to the ISC for the first time in October 2013. They have also begun to speak to a wider audience in forums such as the RUSI,[86] intelligence symposia,[87] academic settings,[88] their own headquarters,[89] and even activist forums[90] in an attempt to explain their role and activities. In that sense, accounts are being given to the public, but the potential for the public to question and respond to these narratives is limited to the elite audience on each occasion. It makes sense for feedback on technical matters to be limited to an informed audience, but some of the issues that have troubled intelligence agencies in recent years relate to ethical questions that could benefit from public debate and scrutiny by lay people. For instance, when and how is it acceptable to use children as intelligence assets? Is it ethical for a government to "seek to alter the ideological views of its citizens as part of its counter-radicalization strategy"?[91] What kinds of response are appropriate to cyberattacks by hostile states? Should Western agencies be engaging in information warfare against authoritarian regimes? These are primarily ethical questions and as such are open to lay people to address.

Overall, the logic of commentary on intelligence accountability suggests that, internally, the agencies are best held to account by individuals with professional experience who can command peer esteem; meanwhile, external oversight is best conducted by groups who have demonstrable independence and rigor. However, each comes with risks and problems that resist easy resolutions. It is important to note that a genuinely unified system of accountability needs to provide clear mechanisms for internal and external account-"receivers" to talk to one another and share information so that a fuller picture of mistakes, inefficiencies, and immorality, as well as excellent performance and virtuous conduct, can be constructed. Furthermore, the sense that the public can or should be excluded from ethical decision-making in intelligence is unlikely to be sustainable and means that the intelligence community is missing out on a potentially fruitful source of innovation and legitimation.

What Is Accountability Meant to Achieve?

This leads one to consider what accountability is for. Intelligence scholars offer subtly different interpretations of its purpose. Maria Caparini sees it as about weighing the efficacy and propriety of the agencies' activities.[92] Ian Leigh opens up these categories and views it as potentially checking "efficiency or effectiveness, legality or proportionality."[93] In both, there is a division between assessing the technical performance of intelligence organizations and making a moral or legal judgment about their ethical or judicial status. A further school of thought draws comparisons between intelligence and the broad field of civil-military relations,[94] identifying the three themes of accountability in this sphere as democratic control, effectiveness, and efficiency.[95]

The latter group tend to be skeptical of the extent to which the effectiveness and efficiency of the intelligence agencies are—or can be—evaluated by accountability forums, especially those external to those organizations, and so focus on democratic control instead.[96] The implication of much of their writing is that accountability's true purpose is to ensure that democratic values and institutions are not being subverted.[97] The power that secrecy and a license to break the law (at least abroad) offers to intelligence officials is considerable, and so accountability is necessary to provide checks on this power and a means of redress for abuse. As a result, intelligence is depicted as an extreme example of the wider tensions in government, between technical expertise, bureaucratic power, and governmental surveillance on the one hand, and individual autonomy, civil rights, and democratic rule by an informed public on the other hand.[98]

In this sense, discussion of intelligence accountability links to the perennial "principal-agent" problem of how a governing actor (the principal) can achieve their goals when the individual or organization tasked with implementing their instructions (the agent) might have their own identity, beliefs, standard operating procedures, and interpretations that affect the result.[99] Thus, the main task of accountability would be to limit any inclination of intelligence and security agents to subvert the will of the principal—either by aligning organizational norms with the intentions of the principal (internal accountability) or providing public affirmation of the principal's instructions (external accountability). What complicates this further is there are at least two principal-agent relationships at play in any discussion of intelligence accountability.[100] On the one hand, the general public is the principal, delegating authority to the state (the agent) to provide for their security (with intelligence a vital component of this).[101] Public accountability is designed to ensure this is done appropriately and effectively. On the other hand, there is also a second-order principal-agent relationship between the government and the agencies. Here, the task of accountability is to ensure these organizations are not acting *ultra vires* (beyond their legally authorized powers) and are carrying out the instructions of the government. This includes acting according to the U.K. civil service code's expressed values of integrity, honesty, objectivity, and impartiality, meaning that officials do not "frustrate the implementation of policies once decisions are taken," or "deceive or knowingly mislead ministers, Parliament, or others."[102]

In devising any system of accountability to cover one or both of these, there is a dilemma over how much autonomy should be afforded to the agent. Governments have to make decisions in secret to avoid handing their opponents an advantage, but this also creates scope to act against the public interest without the public being aware or able to seek redress. There is an argument that officials should be allowed the freedom to use their expertise, knowledge, and judgment to act effectively. This frees agents to use their initiative, but it might also provide a permissive environment for abuse and reduces executive oversight. A balance has to be struck between autonomy and control. Here, secrecy constitutes a substantial obstacle to judging what is appropriate, as principals may not have a full picture of the facts and so could hamper performance, either by being overly restrictive and crippling innovation or by being unduly deferent to expertise. For many practitioners, the need to maintain secrecy trumps the risk of minor performance errors, and so accountability is only intended to avoid the most egregious forms of malpractice—in terms of waste of public money, corruption of political processes, or endangering public safety.[103]

Instead of seeing accountability merely in terms of negative control, it is possible to see it in more positive terms. Viewing accountability as about account-giving and -receiving, rather than "being held to account," we can begin to see practical benefits for all sides. For example, giving an account and receiving feedback offers an opportunity for organizational learning and changes in behavior that might prevent the repetition of mistakes and improve performance. The act of devising an account compels reflection and rationalization of behavior, reminding the official why they are acting, in whose interest they are supposed to do so, and what the boundaries for action are. Thus, the account-giving process reinforces professional norms and links them to the values of the wider society they are seeking to protect.[104] Such accounts could also foster group cohesion by reinforcing a self-identity of a law-abiding and respectable entity acting in the public interest. In this way, it enhances the internal workings of the organization as well as promoting its reputation externally—what Geert Bouckaert and John Halligan describe as "The legitimizing capacity of a good performance story."[105]

The latter point is important, because legitimacy is such a vital aspect to intelligence work.[106] Public trust in the security and intelligence services is essential to many of their key duties, such as counterterrorism, which relies on the cooperation of communities for intelligence-gathering. In communicating the purpose and nature of their activities to scrutiny bodies, accountability can help to reduce tensions between the intelligence services and those communities who are subject to intelligence operations. By offering an account of how and why they are acting, intelligence officials can demonstrate the links between their actions and public goods like community safety and cohesion that benefit those groups as well as wider society.[107] Although the exposure of wrongdoing may affect public trust in those organizations, the overall system is reaffirmed when those who are responsible are visibly asked to account for their behavior and demonstrate how it aligns with the collective good of society.

Similarly, although the technical means of redress that accountability offers might seem to lead to negative publicity, in the long term there are net gains for those organizations in terms of efficiency. By exposing when agencies have broken legal rules, performed inefficiently, been ineffective, or failed to advance the wider public good, accountability regimes allow them to correct their own behavior and improve their performance as a result.

That said, if accountability is to be useful, it should also include scope for offering examples of good practice that other agencies might follow—and have the capacity to reward excellence as well as punish malfeasance.[108] That suggests a more transcendent system of accountability—one that permeates the agencies and operates at multiple levels. Such a move would challenge the tendency to see accountability as a negative activity.[109] It may also move it away from simply being a retrospective process.[110] Rather than accountability as a "response" or "answer," it might begin to be a process of dialogue between the account-giver and -receiver that offered a route to real-time innovation and correction.[111]

To summarize, control is only one of a number of rationales for accountability regimes. Accountability is also an important means of improving the performance of individual officials, upholding collective standards, checking the appropriateness and effectiveness of behavior, and adapting policy in light of the challenges facing those receiving the account. Yet there are difficulties in the account-giving process due to the nature of the work of the intelligence agencies. If secrecy is vital to what they do, simply calling for more openness and transparency is trite and ignores the risks this creates for the public good. Of course, the flipside is that if these agencies are like other governmental bureaucratic organizations (and there is no reason to suggest they are not), secrecy and a lack of accountability at the operational level comes at a likely cost in performance.[112] In the absence of rigorous, open debate, assumptions can become ingrained and bad policies pursued without proper checks or challenges.

The task then is to create a system of accountability for the intelligence services that allows them to function but also ensures their activities are in accordance with domestic values and are performed efficiently and effectively. The logical method of doing so is to accept that some forms of account-giving are necessarily internal and secret, but acknowledge their existence and demonstrate how they link to external and public accountability forums to provide a more holistic system.

New Accountability Challenges

A further difficulty of viewing accountability in terms of control is it implies a linear model of policymaking. The idea of civil servants accountable to ministers, who are in turn accountable to Parliament and ultimately the electorate, fits closely with the Whitehall/Westminster–focused models of governance that traditionally dominated analysis of British government and politics.[113] It suggests a delineable set of policy actions and outcomes, with clear lines of agency and responsibility. In reality, as numerous studies of governance in the United Kingdom have demonstrated, policy neither originates nor is implemented in such a hierarchical fashion. Instead, it is far messier, with policy initiatives emerging across government and the private sector, and at various levels of institutional hierarchies. There is also a strong transnational element to policymaking. Decisions may originate from other actors globally, or through interaction between domestic and international actors, and the way they are implemented is shaped by transnational legal and political arrangements. Thus, governance is "decentred" and the state is fragmented, since a plethora of actors decide, interpret, implement, and contest policy.[114]

It could be argued that intelligence is different from normal policymaking, as secrecy means that the executive retains control over much of the policy process. Yet secrecy also carries the potential to obscure the practice of intelligence from other tiers in the hierarchy. Moreover, thanks to technological advances in digital communications and surveillance, a far greater number of agencies within government now produce and consume intelligence. That means a denser and broader network of intelligence practice. Intelligence cooperation with other states has also widened and deepened, particularly as part of global efforts to combat terrorism, supported by international agreements, such as UN Security Council Resolution 1373.

Therefore, our understanding of accountability should perhaps move away from linear understandings of control and instead reflect the reality of a more dynamic intelligence policy environment. Focusing on how accounts are rendered, via processes of account-giving and -receiving, rather than just lines of management responsibility, opens up our understanding of how intelligence is understood and practiced across government, and between U.K. government agencies and their counterparts abroad. It also encourages more creative ways to scrutinize this activity, beyond the narrow horizons of judicial or legislative oversight.

A second challenge to current understandings of accountability lies in the rapid and transformative impact of new technologies on intelligence practice. The human element of intelligence work, not just in terms of data collection but also analysis, is increasingly giving way to automation and artificial intelligence. Thus, analysis of internet traffic makes use of algorithms that search for predefined behavior likely to indicate criminality or security threats.[115] Importantly, artificial intelligence is also coming into play in this regard, with machines learning and adapting to feedback in ways that go beyond the original human-derived parameters. A 2018 Chatham House report sets out the impact of this shift:

> For all of human history, politics has been fundamentally driven by conscious human action and the collective actions and interactions of humans within networks and organizations. Now, advances in artificial intelligence (AI) hold out the prospect of a fundamental change in this arrangement: the idea of a non-human entity having specific agency could create radical change in our understanding of politics at the widest levels.[116]

A particular problem for intelligence accountability lies in identifying the responsible actor in each case. Thus, if suspect activity is wrongly detected and leads to serious human consequences, this may be caused by a machine that is unable to account for its actions. In addition, should this be the result of artificial intelligence, human operators may not have even been aware of the processes that led to the outcome and so can deflect responsibility, leaving the victim unable to seek redress.

To overcome this issue, commentators have advocated mixed human-AI arrangements, sometimes described as "centaurs," whereby "the machine can process enormous quantities of data quickly while the human can spot-check and correct where necessary."[117] But this might not be practicable, depending on the quantity of data involved and the complexity of the analysis undertaken. One of the hoped-for advantages of using technology was that it could eradicate errors caused by human prejudices; however, when artificial intelligence systems have been deployed to sift data and make judgments, they have been found to replicate the biases of human society.[118] Amnesty International and Access Now launched a declaration in May 2018 designed to protect the "rights to equality and non-discrimination in machine learning systems."[119] To overcome the potential biases in machine learning systems, the declaration advocates the "active participation of, and meaningful consultation with, a diverse community to ensure that machine learning systems are designed and used in ways that respect non-discrimination, equality, and other human rights."[120]

The problem lies in the fact that current official mechanisms of accountability are, as noted above, elite-driven, and as such do not reflect the diversity of the population at large. Meaningful consultation with diverse groups is not being undertaken in this area by the intelligence community (though some intercommunal dialogue occurs in other areas, such as over the PREVENT strategy). Moreover, since accountability is often conceived in terms of linear models of decisionmaking, leading to a retrospective punitive judgment, existing accountability mechanisms are ill-equipped to grapple with the nonlinearity of AI and other technological issues. If a fuller understanding of accountability was used, encompassing "rendering account"—account-giving—as well as "holding to account," this might open up space for dialogue between intelligence officials and cyber-experts from other fields, and a recognition that AI creates ethical dilemmas for producers and consumers.

A final category of problem for intelligence accountability, and one that is increasingly apparent, is whistleblowing. As noted above, technology and social changes have combined to make it easier to leak sensitive material and distribute it widely through online platforms. Perhaps the most infamous example for the United Kingdom was Edward Snowden's 2013 revelations about Britain's interception of communications data in cooperation with the United States. Yet despite this leak leading to three major reviews of intelligence practice and new legislation, it is curious that neither the reviews nor the Investigatory Powers Act that followed made any effort to reconsider the current procedures for whistleblowing. It has been disputed whether Edward Snowden is a whistleblower or simply a traitor for leaking secret intelligence; however, his actions undeniably led to substantial debate over intelligence practices. They also demonstrated the challenges faced by the agencies in maintaining secrecy—particularly when it comes to programs that involve interagency cooperation. In his first report, the investigatory powers commissioner argued: "in the post-Snowden world, the security and law enforcement agencies can no longer expect to work in the shadows, in the sense that material which can properly be made public should be widely available for scrutiny."[121] Thus, the commissioner seems to concede the public benefit that flowed from Snowden's actions.

The 2015 RUSI report did mention some of the internal procedures for staff to express concern about what they are asked to do. MI5, SIS, and GCHQ each have a dedicated ethics counsellor to whom (according to the report) "ethical concerns can be raised and discussed freely" by staff.[122] In addition, a staff counsellor is available to officials, described as "an external appointee who works across the three agencies" and who "is a point of contact for any members of the security and intelligence agencies who have anxieties relating to the work of their service which it has not been possible to allay through the ordinary processes of management or staff relations."[123] The staff counsellor's function was elaborated in a written statement by David Cameron in May 2016, as he appointed Julian Miller to the post: "The post holder is available to be consulted by any member of the Agencies regarding matters of conscience about the work of their service, or a personal grievance or other problem which has not been resolved internally."[124] The counsellor apparently produces reports on at least an annual basis to the prime minister and relevant heads of department.[125] The RUSI report also makes reference to a whistleblowing policy "by which employees can raise any concerns over perceived malpractice or impropriety" but does not elaborate on how this operates.[126]

The workings of these three mechanisms of account-giving have not been made public, with the exception of occasional stories related to concerns expressed by officials, as reproduced in the ISC's Annual Report in 2009.[127] They have also attracted academic criticism for being too close to management structures or, in the case of the staff counsellor, operating more as an "agony uncle" than a rigorous means of highlighting concerns and having them addressed in a way that might change policy.[128] The lack of transparency about the identity of the staff counsellor (with the exception of David Cameron's parliamentary answer in 2016) and their function, leaves an information vacuum, which does not serve to reassure the public that officials will be encouraged to raise concerns without repercussions for their career or safety. Important questions can be raised about their operation: should the counsellor maintain confidentiality to protect the source or do they have a responsibility to report wrongdoing? Is anonymity possible for those reporting concerns? Would it be enough to feed complaints up the internal chain of command, or, if the policy itself is wrong, should they communicate this to an external third party?

A further set of questions arise when it comes to how counsellors link with their internal and external counterparts. What right would judicial commissioners have to access any information provided to counsellors? Who holds judicial commissioners accountable if their approval of operations were to be reckless or wrong? In extreme cases of malpractice, when would an official be justified in circumventing these procedures and notifying scrutiny bodies, such as the ISC, their MP, or the media?

I explore the workings of the counsellor system in chapter 3 through interviews with practitioners. For now, it is worth noting alternative means by which whistleblowers are encouraged in other spheres. In recent decades, the United States has encouraged corporate whistleblowing in the finance world through a series of regulations and laws designed to "express a decidedly moral view of whistleblowers as allies in the fight against corporate fraud, bribery, and corruption."[129] This even went so far as providing substantial monetary incentives, such as the 2010 Dodd-Frank Act, which stipulated that whistleblowers could receive a proportion of the monetary sanctions imposed on those found guilty, with the average bounty expected "to be well in the range of $2 million to $5 million dollars."[130] In the medical profession, Chanel Watson and Tom O'Conner have noted that doctors have been investigated by the General Medical Council for not "blowing the whistle" and reporting poor patient care—indicating this is a professional duty that carries the threat of sanction or even dismissal if not fulfilled.[131] These are examples of strong regimes that incentivize whistleblowing but neither approach has been tried in the U.K. intelligence context. The nearest the intelligence and security agencies have come to embracing whistleblowing as an ethical duty was when Eliza Manningham-Buller, director general of the Security Service, issued a circular titled "Ethics and the Security Service" in 2006, stating: "I urge staff to say if they have qualms. The idea that airing concern on the proper channels risks damage to career is a myth."[132] Yet the reporting mechanisms at this time were largely in-house, and so it is hard to evaluate their effectiveness.

Organizations can often be resistant to change and become entrenched in their habits, at the risk of ignoring important warnings about the need to reappraise their actions. At times, it may take an outsider to offer the requisite level of detachment to look at patterns of behavior afresh and make a moral judgment about appropriateness against wider social values. As an example, Philip Zimbardo notes that in his infamous Stanford prison experiment in 1971 (whereby college students were assigned roles as prisoners and guards to see how far they altered their behavior to fit these positions) the participants began to engage in psychological and sexual abuse, but he and his fellow investigators were so wrapped up in their observations that they failed to stop the study until his romantic partner visited the facility and was horrified by the goings-on.[133] The question is whether the intelligence and security agencies have equivalent individuals in place to act as a moral check on their everyday practices. The staff counsellor is external to the organization, and so on that level they might be sufficiently detached to offer a fresh perspective on any activities reported to them—though to be appointed to this position they must have had some familiarity with intelligence and security work, and so would also have the status of insider compared with a lay person. They also appear to act more as a sounding board than an inquisitor.

Incorporating whistleblowing to external bodies within the official accountability framework carries its own risks. Individuals might raise complaints for egoistic reasons—to self-identify as mavericks or heroes in a corrupt system—rather than as a genuine effort to effect policy change. In the latter cases, it may be difficult or impossible to assuage the complainant's concerns, and trying to do so could undermine the overall efficiency of the organization. It also threatens the integrity of the secret intelligence system. Secrecy may be required for collective reasons, and individuals, unless very senior, will often hold a narrow personal perspective that prevents them from accurately judging what is safe to share with other parties externally. In that sense, whistleblowing could endanger colleagues' safety or even lives. One can also imagine recourse to external parties undermining the social fabric of intelligence agencies. Secret organizations rely on their members working closely together, exercising discretion and trust. That also arguably extends to offering colleagues the opportunity to correct negative behavior themselves rather than be compelled to by external actors. As Geoffrey Hunt puts it, whistleblowers are "caught in this contest of accountabilities—a hero to the public and a troublemaker, even a deviant, to the organization."[134] Yet, as noted above, "accountabilities are shifting, or can be shifted, to encompass a wider arena of stakeholders."[135] Senior officials are now giving accounts in public and to external bodies. If other members of the intelligence machinery perceive these to be inaccurate or misleading, they may feel a divided loyalty between their organization and the public interest. Furthermore, it is worth noting the personal costs of not whistleblowing. In other professions, this carries legal penalties and psychological costs to individuals' welfare.[136] Given the technological and social changes in intelligence work in the digital age, the intelligence machinery is going to need to give more attention to how it enables its staff to consider the ethical implications of their work and perhaps blow the whistle on malpractice and unethical policies in a safe manner. As will be seen in chapter 3, more space has been opened up to ethical debate and the expression of dissent among personnel, but there is still a lack of coherent avenues for whistleblowing.

Nor can this simply be resolved through legislation. In the United States, there is a relatively dense legislative framework to encourage whistleblowers and protect them from retribution, starting with the Intelligence Community Whistleblower Protection Act (ICWPA) of 1998.[137] Yet when an intelligence official followed the correct procedures in making a complaint against President Donald Trump in September 2019 through the inspector general for the intelligence community, the whistleblower faced a campaign of harassment and vilification. The president called for the person's name to be revealed on a number of occasions, accused the person of making up "false stories," and implied that he or she should face retribution.[138] The person's identity was also possibly leaked in a tweet from the president's son.[139] This is a reminder that the right political culture needs to be in place—one that acknowledges the public benefit of whistleblowing—if those who do so through the proper channels are to be protected.

To recap, from the above discussion it is apparent that the accountability of public bodies involves both soliciting information about their behavior and compelling them to explain and justify their actions. In the world of intelligence, these processes are restricted, elite-focused, largely retrospective, focus on policy more than practice, and apply different standards of scrutiny depending on whether the activity takes place domestically or overseas. The need for secrecy inhibits the space for account-giving as well as the range of people who would be suitable recipients of such accounts; however, there is more to accountability than just the formal structures of reporting. Accounts are shared, justifications offered, and actions judged within organizations, as well as across Whitehall and beyond, including public and private actors.[140] Therefore, organizational culture and wider social norms and practices come into play. In the following chapter, the accounts that have been solicited by formal accountability mechanisms will be explored and the issues they raise delineated. While an increasing level of formal scrutiny has offered a much richer understanding of what the U.K. intelligence and security agencies do, it also underlines the limits to such forms of accountability.

TWO

Scrutinizing the U.K. Intelligence Machinery

This chapter explores the main criticisms of the U.K. national intelligence machinery and the primary accountability challenges that have arisen in the United Kingdom over the last two decades. In doing so, it aims to establish a picture of what oversight bodies, the media, and informed commentators prioritize when it comes to holding the intelligence and security agencies to account. Echoing the discussion of accountability theory in the previous chapter, it is apparent that external scrutinizers analyze accountability in terms of the effectiveness, efficiency, or ethics of the intelligence and security services, with different groups emphasizing different aspects of their performance. Effectiveness can be further subdivided into two parts, one looking at the policies initiated, and the other at the methods used to implement them. The analysis that follows is therefore divided into four categories of accountability problems identified by the various inquiries and oversight bodies. In terms of effectiveness, we have two parts: political issues (including poor coordination between agencies, misinterpretation of intelligence, and failure to anticipate threats) and operational issues (including problems with the handling, production, and analysis of intelligence). Efficiency is analyzed in relation to accounting issues (including poor record-keeping, waste, and misallocation of resources). Lastly, the ethical concerns over intelligence and security practices (ranging from the treatment of detainees to cooperation with international partners on surveillance and rendition, breaches of the Official Secrets Act, and agent-running) are considered. These are of varying severity and importance.

Although the focus of this chapter is largely on problems highlighted by accountability forums, that is not meant to suggest that the general level of performance of the U.K. intelligence and security agencies is poor. Indeed, the commissioners and the ISC repeatedly emphasize the opposite. In his final report, Sir Mark Waller, the intelligence services commissioner, stated: "I would like to record that the United Kingdom is extremely fortunate with its intelligence agencies. They combine an extremely high level of operational competence with a collaborative approach and a respect for the law which makes them trusted and respected internationally."[1] This sentiment has been echoed by previous commissioners.[2] The ISC presages critical comments with statements such as "Whilst this Report includes a number of criticisms and concerns relating to the U.K. Intelligence Community, we would not wish these points to overshadow the essential and excellent work that the Agencies have undertaken."[3] That the individuals tasked with scrutinizing these agencies retain a high opinion of them is perhaps indicative that the agencies' overall standard of performance is high. Furthermore, a focus on negative aspects here is not meant to project the sense of accountability as a wholly negative exercise in fault-finding. Hopefully, this impression will be balanced out by later chapters that explore how practitioners utilize accountability to improve their performance.

Political Issues

The most damaging political issue with regard to intelligence in recent memory relates to the decision to go to war in Iraq in 2003.[4] Intelligence was a vital component of the government's assessment of the threat Iraq represented. The series of inquiries held after 2003 exonerated the government and the agencies of acting in bad faith, but highlighted important errors of political judgment and process. In particular, the Chilcot report noted "the ingrained belief of the government and the intelligence community that Saddam Hussein's regime retained chemical and biological warfare capabilities . . . and was pursuing an active and successful policy of deception and concealment."[5] Once this opinion had formed, no formal reassessment took place of this assumption, even when Dr. Hans Blix published a report on March 7, 2003, indicating that Iraq was cooperating more substantively with the UNMOVIC inspections and no evidence of proscribed activities had been found.[6]

Perhaps most important for trust in the intelligence and security agencies, policymakers not only relied on faulty intelligence but used it publicly to build the case for war. In September 2002, six months before the invasion, the government produced a dossier, with a foreword by the prime minister, outlining their assessment of Iraq's weapons of mass destruction capabilities.[7] This was put together using Joint Intelligence Committee assessments and was overseen by the JIC chairman, John Scarlett; however, the Hutton inquiry revealed that this was not intended to be a neutral presentation of the evidence. Rather, Hutton noted that: "Mr. Alastair Campbell made it clear to Mr. Scarlett on behalf of the prime minister that 10 Downing Street wanted the dossier to be worded to make as strong a case as possible in relation to the threat posed by Saddam Hussein's WMD, and 10 Downing Street made written suggestions to Mr. Scarlett as to changes in the wording of the draft dossier that would strengthen it."[8] The Butler report in 2004 stated that "judgments in the dossier went to (although not beyond) the outer limits of the intelligence available," but was highly critical of the fact that "the limitations of the intelligence underlying some of its judgments were not made sufficiently clear.[9]

Tony Blair was singled out for blame for his portrayal of the evidence to the House of Commons as "extensive, detailed, and authoritative," when in reality it was portrayed by the intelligence community as "sporadic and patchy."[10] Blair's approach to government was highly informal, and the effect of this was evident in the lack of rigor with which ministers considered intelligence policy. The ISC frequently complained that the Ministerial Committee on the Intelligence Services did not meet at all between 1995 and 2002.[11] Yet ministers are not solely to blame for errors in this era. Buried within the reports were implied criticisms of the intelligence community. Given that the JIC chairman was overseeing the dossier, the

Chilcot inquiry concluded: "The JIC itself should have made that position clear . . . The process of seeking the JIC's views, through Mr. Scarlett, on the text of the Foreword shows that No. 10 expected the JIC to raise any concerns it had."[12] With regard to Blair's infamous claim in the foreword that Iraq's WMD could be "ready within 45 minutes of an order to use them,"[13] Chilcot placed some of the blame for this report on the head of the Secret Intelligence Service, arguing: "Sir Richard Dearlove's personal intervention, and its urgency, gave added weight to a report that had not been properly evaluated and would have coloured the perception of Ministers and senior officials. The report should have been treated with caution."[14] The Butler and Chilcot inquiries were also critical of the failure to share this information with members of the defense intelligence staff in the Ministry of Defence, as well as the delays in reporting to ministers that intelligence had been withdrawn as unreliable.[15]

The legacy of these errors is that government statements on intelligence are now met with considerable skepticism. This has important implications for foreign and security policy.[16] Debates on military intervention include frequent references to Iraq and implied mistrust of intelligence claims.[17] Most notably, the government's attempt to argue for military action in Syria in 2013, based on intelligence reports that the Assad government was responsible for a chemical weapons attack on civilians, resulted in the first parliamentary defeat of a government motion on the use of force since the 1780s. It is possible the Iraq analogy has begun to lose its resonance. When in 2018 the Labor Party spokesperson responded to allegations of Russian involvement in the Skripal poisoning by saying "I think obviously the government has access to information and intelligence on this matter, which others don't; however, also there's a history in relation to WMD and intelligence, which is problematic to put it mildly," he was roundly criticized.[18] Yet this shows Iraq is still a reference point for those skeptical of the intelligence and security agencies.

The national intelligence machinery instituted a number of reforms in subsequent years, which were inspired by the need to correct political failings. The United Kingdom now has a national security advisor and a National Security Council made up of key ministers who are supposed to meet and discuss security matters, including intelligence, in a more rigorous fashion than the "sofa government" of the Blair years. In response to the Butler report's recommendation, the JIC chair position increased in seniority, being placed on a par with the agency heads; however, the ISC expressed concern when this role was conflated at various times with the security and intelligence coordinator and later the professional head of intelligence analysis, since these posts were supposed to provide a challenge function to intelligence assumptions.[19] To avoid the errors that led to the forty-five-minute claim achieving such prominence, SIS stated to the ISC that they had "now appointed a senior officer to be responsible for the accuracy (in terms of both validation and correct evaluation of the product) of intelligence reports issued by the SIS. In order to guarantee impartiality, this senior officer reports to two different members of the SIS board, only one of whom is responsible for operations."[20] Thus, a more robust means of checking the reliability of intelligence and avoiding undue political influence has been instituted at a bureaucratic level.

The dominant place that Iraq occupies in the intelligence imagination has arguably led to other political failings in intelligence being overlooked. For instance, blame for not preventing the attacks on the United States on 9/11 usually falls on the U.S. intelligence community, but it remains the single deadliest terrorist attack on British citizens as well, with sixty-seven killed. In the subsequent ISC report in 2002, the committee notes: "The Agencies have told us that they had no intelligence forewarning them specifically about the . . . attacks."[21] It goes on to conclude: "with hindsight . . . the scale of the threat and the vulnerability of Western states to terrorists with this degree of sophistication and a total disregard for their own lives was not understood."[22] Yet the committee does not offer any censure for this omission—or recommendations for better "horizon scanning" of future threats.

In 2006, U.K. forces deployed to Helmand Province, Afghanistan, to support the NATO mission and extend government control over the area. Although SIS and Defence Intelligence staff did apparently conduct assessments of the threat environment,[23] the number of troops deployed was very small and they were installed in company-sized groups that were unable to establish control over territory. In addition, they found themselves confronting a sizeable insurgency that took them by surprise. Theo Farrell has described this as "an extraordinary intelligence failure, especially as the U.S. ambassador in Kabul and the commander of Combined Forces Command, Afghanistan, were both warning of a rising insurgency in 2006 and predicting that the Taliban would 'strike hard before NATO could become well established on the ground.' "[24] In other words, the British government put troops in harm's way without properly assessing the risks. This intervention would cost 451 U.K. military and civilian lives.[25] Yet one would search in vain for any reference to this intelligence failing in the ISC's reports.

The outbreak of the Arab Spring and the meteoric rise of Islamic State also came as a surprise to intelligence agencies. In relation to the first, the ISC suggested that such events were hard to predict but questioned why the agencies were unable to anticipate how developments would unfold and attributed this to the decision to reduce intelligence resources in the region. This was supported by evidence from the director of GCHQ, who noted: "the Arab nations were one of the few areas where we were planning to draw down our effort pretty well comprehensively."[26] The ISC raised the question whether "the fact that they did not realise that the unrest would spread so rapidly across the Arab world demonstrates a lack of understanding about the region," which is striking, given the geographical proximity and political importance of the Maghreb to Europe.[27]

When it came to a lack of foresight of the rise of Islamic State, the ISC failed to mention this as an intelligence failing in any of its reports; despite a debate in U.S. circles on why the rise of ISIS was not anticipated, with some attributing it to an emphasis on signals intelligence over human intelligence sources.[28] It is curious that no similar soul-searching appears to have taken place within the accountability mechanisms of the United Kingdom—even though this resulted in the deaths of a number of British citizens taken as hostages and gave rise to new dilemmas about the use of lethal force against British terrorist suspects abroad.[29]

In short, the experience of Iraq may have led to improvements in the political coordination of intelligence machinery, but the agencies have a long-running problem with providing anticipatory intelligence on security threats, which persists to this day. The ISC implicitly shifted the blame for this to ministers in its annual report for 2003–04: "A great deal has been spoken about 'intelligence failures.' The U.K. intelligence and security Agencies collect secret intelligence on threats only when they are authorised to collect it."[30] As seen above, ministers failed to properly consider intelligence policy at times. However, this has to be a dialogue between ministers and agencies, since it is the agencies that have the assets that should give warning of imminent developments. This is underlined by the ISC's following comment: "Secret intelligence will never give complete certainty about all events in the world, but it is important that threats are identified as early as possible . . . If . . . this does not happen and an unexpected event occurs, people will accuse the Agencies of having failed."[31] What it does not add is that such accusations may be justified. It is one thing to issue a warning and not have it heeded, but to misread the threat environment, as happened over 9/11, Iraq, Afghanistan, the Arab Spring, the threat from Russia, and the rise of Islamic State, is arguably a poor record—even if balanced against the successful assessments of North Korea and Libya.[32] In its commentary on the performance of the intelligence agencies, the ISC focused strongly on Iraq but missed a lot of other problems in the way intelligence was used to assess political developments.

Operational Issues

The above discussion has relevance when it comes to criticisms of operational performance. Lack of foresight is sometimes attributed to the downsizing of the agencies after the Cold War.[33] A shift in approach was discernible from "intelligence in depth," with a high level of spare capacity, to more reactive "just in time" supply of information. This move was a logical step when dealing with less static foes than during the Cold War. However, it meant that deep subject and regional expertise was lost and had to be reconstituted quickly in response to emerging crises. Thus, during the Afghanistan campaign in 2001, individuals were brought back from retirement, in one case for the second time, to fill knowledge gaps.[34]

The streamlining of reporting processes in the 1990s was also blamed for a lack of challenge of assumptions, which had serious consequences when it came to the Iraq War in 2003.[35] For intelligence collection and analysis to be useful, it has to link closely with the needs of policymakers; however, at the same time, analysts have to maintain a level of distance from government pressures so they can analyze the truth and meaning of intelligence in a rigorous manner. Without mechanisms to check and challenge interpretations, such as through "red teams," or periodic reassessment from first principles, ideas can become entrenched and intelligence filtered to support preconceptions that may no longer fit with reality. As various inquiries have shown, there were major errors in the collection, verification, and assessment of intelligence by U.K. agencies prior to the Iraq War. These, in part, derived from policymakers asking the wrong questions. There is a subtle difference between asking whether a threat exists and asking for intelligence of a threat. In the first case, the possibility is left open to discount the threat's existence, whereas in the second, the challenge is to collate information that solidifies it. Nevertheless, it was also a failing of the organizations themselves if they did not have in place sufficient internal ways of verifying their intelligence and questioning assumptions.

After the invasion of Iraq in 2003, a mixed picture emerged of how far the intelligence agencies succeeded in providing reliable intelligence during the occupation. In evidence to the Chilcot inquiry, an SIS official argued that the Service had had "a pretty good war in terms of providing intelligence support for British forces in the South . . . the battle for Basra . . . That was an intelligence-led success."[36] Yet military personnel highlighted problems with the quality of intelligence after the initial military victory. One commander noted: "All of our intelligence assets were looking at the Iraqi forces. What they were not looking at was the infrastructure, and . . . when we arrived in there, I was amazed . . . that it was completely broken."[37] In a military lessons study on Operation Telic, endorsed by the chiefs of staff in 2010, it was asserted that "there had been a lack of an enduring intelligence picture for 'at least the first four years' of the campaign."[38] Given the problems with intelligence over Iraq, it is striking how few lessons were apparently learned before forces were committed again in Afghanistan in 2006. Senior British military figures were so concerned about the lack of intelligence on Helmand Province prior to that later deployment that they paused operational planning, only to be forced to resume it for political reasons.[39]

As many of the scrutiny bodies note, collecting intelligence in hostile environments, such as Saddam Hussein's Iraq or Afghanistan, is difficult. Nevertheless, one might have expected more reflection by the agencies about whether sufficient resources were allocated to these efforts and how far intelligence failures were the result of the hardness of the target or poor operational performance. The ISC may have been restricted at times in its ability to criticize operational effectiveness due to the fact that its remit specifically excludes ongoing operations—unless the agencies volunteer information themselves.[40] Yet such a stance is problematic, given the length of the Iraq and Afghanistan campaigns, and precludes the possibility of evaluating performance in a way that could rescue failing operations or improve concurrent operations in other theaters.

Former intelligence officers provide a robust defense of the performance of SIS when it came to military operations. Of the Iraq invasion in 2003, one asserts: "talk to Robin Brims about the battle for Basra and he will tell you that that was an intelligence-led battle. You talk to some of the squaddies who went into the Faw Peninsula and all that, and they will tell you that we were telling them where the Iraqi armored columns were well in advance."[41] The picture gleaned from SIS is that intelligence was strong and played an important role in military success. When the occupation later began to fail, this was attributed to some military commanders not heeding intelligence advice.

In the case of Britain's intervention in Helmand Province under Operation Herrick, SIS personnel describe this as a "vanity project by the military" and assert that they were not involved in the early decisionmaking process: "Nobody consulted us. Nobody asked us what intelligence we had and did we think this was a good idea? I have to say it did not take very long to come to the conclusion that it probably was not a very good idea but, by that point, the die was cast."[42] As such, the intelligence service was left to try and catch up, providing "the best possible state of readiness to support them with the intelligence that they are going to need."[43] One issue in gauging the effectiveness of SIS when it comes to providing anticipatory intelligence is in the way they define themselves. One former SIS officer asserts: "MI6 is a highly operational service. It is not an analytical service. A lot of other services are more analytical rather than operational."[44] In that reading, it would perhaps be the job of other groups, in the National Security Secretariat or Defence Intelligence, to do the analysis of threat required.

If failures of intelligence in Iraq and Afghanistan are, on balance, attributed more to political than operational errors, the same cannot arguably be said of domestic terrorist attacks. In their report on the Woolwich murder of Lee Rigby, the ISC highlighted instances where MI5 missed chances to investigate connections between the killers and other political extremists that were under surveillance. For instance, MI5's failure to request billing data for the landline at Michael Adebowale's home address in January 2013 meant they missed the opportunity to understand the extent of his links with a subject of interest "ECHO."[45] Their focus on networks was also seen as problematic, as it meant that not enough significance was attached to individuals who repeatedly cropped up in connection with different subjects of interest, albeit in a peripheral role.[46]

This case revealed significant problems with reporting, which were highlighted across a number of annual ISC reports.[47] It may be tempting to view this as a bureaucratic tactic to restrict information to the ISC—as was alleged to have been the case when it came to recording mistreatment of detainees in Detainee Contact Reports. In its 2018 follow-up report on this issue, the ISC quotes an SIS officer, suggesting:

> whilst it may be SIS culture to record everything, there were situations like this where people would say something was "not for the write-up." He told us that there "was quite an emphasis then on not putting things in writing . . . Because presumably they didn't want the ISC to read the documents later. . . . it wasn't as if the basic attitude to record-keeping had been abandoned; it was more that the more complicated stuff that was at the fringes of normal was not being recorded."[48]

By contrast, the agencies' official accounts attributed poor record-keeping to operational pressures, arguing:

> record-keeping was inadequate during this time. So the absolute imperative was to find and report information pertaining to threats, terrorist intelligence. And the thing that haunts an SIS officer more than anything else is failing to report something that subsequently proves important to stopping a bomb going off. So that will have been the absolute priority. In that environment we did not do what we would do now as a matter of institutional reflex, which is also record all of the details of each detainee interaction. That's something that has completely changed.[49]

To the lay person, recording all the details of an interaction would seem vital in case extraneous information proved to be relevant later on. For instance, in evaluating the weight to give intelligence, the extent to which an individual was under duress would seem an important factor. If poor record-keeping was in part a defense mechanism against future oversight, this would have had operational implications.[50] Moreover, inadequate record-keeping and search capabilities seem to persist beyond the pressures of working abroad. The ISC states that "there is very little in the documents seen by the Committee recording regular meetings between Ministers and the Heads of the Agencies."[51] A 2004 staff survey commissioned by the prime minister recorded only fifteen out of eighty-three incidents of concern subsequently identified, and ISC search requests for their 2007 report into rendition were later shown to be seriously incomplete. Criticizing the Security Service, the ISC argued, "whilst MI5 might keep adequate records of what they do, they are not always easy to search and retrieve,"[52] and the Director General Jonathan Evans admitted, "there was a fault with our processes or record-keeping." SIS eventually provided further information but also added the caveat: "it cannot be ruled out that searches carried out using different search parameters, for example, in connection with any future court proceedings in the U.K., might unearth additional information."[53]

Again, this might seem like obfuscation; however, problems in record-keeping and reporting are evident even when it goes against the agencies' interest. For example, SIS attracted criticism for not responding to an email from an officer in the field regarding the treatment of one of the Woolwich killers, Michael Adebolajo, by Kenyan authorities. It was later discovered that a reply had been sent, but poor record-keeping did not reveal this at the time of the inquiry. Moreover, the agencies did report errors promptly to the commissioners when they came to light.[54] Nevertheless, the fact that these agencies were unable to address issues of record-keeping despite repeated criticisms over more than a decade is both an indictment of their operational performance and perhaps leads one to question the power of the commissioners and the ISC to hold them to account.

Another operational failing identified by the ISC, which may have contributed to poor performance, was in training. The ISC's report into mistreatment of detainees asserted that personnel "lacked the experience and training necessary in the complex situations that deployed staff faced in dealing with detainees in Afghanistan, Iraq, Guantanamo, and elsewhere."[55] In an astonishing admission, the chief of SIS wrote to the prime minister in 2014, acknowledging that SIS officers "had no training, no policy, and no guidance on conducting detainee interviews, and very little on operations leading to detention."[56] A kind interpretation of this omission might be the novelty of the operating environment after 9/11, but the ISC states:

"By the time of the deployment to Iraq in 2003, there was no excuse for the lack of training and guidance available to deployed personnel—there was both time to prepare and an understanding of the operating environment gleaned from the earlier deployments."[57] This is a serious operational failing. Conducting detainee interviews is a highly specialized skill that requires proper training to elicit intelligence. It is apparent from these accounts that the agencies only introduced such arrangements when they came under external pressure.[58] This supports Peter Gill's contention that "Recruitment, training, codes of ethics . . . are all issues requiring attention. If left simply to 'insiders,' the issues may be dealt with from the mind-set of law and rights as minimal standards for practice or, worse, as minimal standards for reporting on practice."[59] However, it is important to note that internal pressure was also being exerted at this time. Officers on the ground repeatedly called for advice on how to respond to instances of mistreatment by liaison forces. It is perhaps more accurate to see dual pressures from above and below compelling senior officers to institute changes.

In addition to these failings, the operational performance of the agencies came into question in light of a number of intelligence fiascos that brought embarrassment to the government. In 2006, British spies were allegedly caught on camera by the Russian state security service, the FSB, transmitting electronic information to a false rock by a grass verge, which was then obtained by the Russians, who broadcast the names of the individuals in question and arrested a Russian citizen.[60] At the time, U.K. officials issued blanket denials, but the story was later confirmed in 2012 by Jonathan Powell, the chief of staff to the then–prime minister, Tony Blair, who admitted, "they had us bang to rights."[61] In 2010, SIS suffered embarrassment when its program to reach out to Taliban leaders in Afghanistan and sow division in their ranks was undermined by the revelation that one of the individuals they had been negotiating with—and whom they had introduced to the Afghan president, Hamid Karzai—was actually a grocer from Quetta.[62]

An equally embarrassing blunder occurred during Britain's intervention in Libya in March 2011. An intelligence team of two MI6 and six SAS personnel was deployed by helicopter at night into Eastern Libya, tasked with making contact with rebel forces fighting Colonel Qaddafi; however, they were immediately arrested by those forces, who had not been forewarned about their entry into the country. A Libyan representative was quoted as saying, "We don't want new enemies, but this is no way to make contact."[63] The U.K. opposition spokesperson was able to make political capital from this in the House of Commons.[64] After a few days of diplomatic negotiation, the individuals were released, but this incident was seen by the ISC as having "serious practical and diplomatic consequences" and was attributed to pressure from ministers for intelligence leading to "a lack of operational planning that we would not have expected from SIS and other participants."[65]

The government did praise the overall performance of the agencies in the Libya case, with the foreign secretary arguing that "their ability to turn the antennae in the right direction was quite remarkable, and the volume of material produced by GCHQ on Libya was colossal: up to the point of an entire full red box every day for me to read of GCHQ reports on Libya."[66] Yet having planned to downgrade their intelligence presence in North Africa, the agencies were clearly having to catch up, and SIS "acknowledged that they had been 'unable to provide detailed reporting on [the] Tunisia and Egypt crises.' "[67]

As far as the political fallout went, these fiascos were contained, and the intelligence agencies did not suffer lasting reputational damage. Nevertheless, in the case of Libya, poor decisions about allocation of resources clearly had negative impacts on outcomes. The agencies reacted in a timely manner and recovered sufficiently, so much so that the minister responsible was happy with their performance. The government asserted that a thorough review was conducted by SIS into the operational fiasco in Libya and recommendations about the "management of risk" were implemented.[68] In other words, lessons were supposedly learned. However, the agencies clearly did not accept that the Arab Spring should have been anticipated and therefore it was wrong to pull resources from the region. The government argued: "The various factors that eventually resulted in the Arab Spring were well known to the intelligence community and other observers. What was not possible to predict in detail, however, was the precise timing of events, nor the way that they unfolded."[69] Rather, the agencies were seen as having been tasked by the "Priorities for Intelligence Coverage" set by the National Security Council and Joint Intelligence Committee and so could only respond reactively to events and issues outside this framework.[70] The economic context of austerity would exacerbate this trend, with the ISC concluding that cuts to Defence Intelligence's resources and staff meant it was "likely that even greater risk will have to be taken when reacting to the next crisis than was the case with the Libya campaign. This is an unsatisfactory position."[71]

A final element of operational error extends beyond the intelligence agencies to the wider community of security organizations using intelligence in the United Kingdom. In the annex to their reports, the interception of communications commissioner notes recurring problems with the transcription of telephone numbers and IP addresses, leading to devices being seized, individuals questioned, and, at times, people arrested based on wrong information.[72] Given the number of public bodies involved in intercepting communications, the instance of errors reported is low (ninety-six public authorities are listed as making communications data requests in 2016, but only twenty-nine serious errors were identified).[73] Nevertheless, the consequences can be extremely serious. When an incorrect day and month were typed into an IP resolution request—designed to identify the Internet subscriber responsible for criminal behavior, authorities initiated safeguarding procedures and separated two children from their parents for a weekend until the error was revealed. One individual who suffered from such an error, Nigel Lang, was arrested and questioned by Hertfordshire police in 2011 and had to live away from his child for a number of weeks before he was found to be innocent. He described the emotional impact as severe: "I'm ill because of it, suffering from post-traumatic stress disorder. My personality has changed. I'm more angry, I struggle with a lack of sleep and am hyper-vigilant around people, being paranoid that people are talking about me."[74] The expansion of the number of public bodies who can access personal data in recent years means that such errors are likely to become more frequent.

Accounting Errors

As noted above, a key source of complaint about the performance of the intelligence community in the United Kingdom related to record-keeping. One would expect accurate record management to be a core requirement of any effective intelligence machinery. In addition to the ISC's continual criticisms, the agencies were also rebuked by the coroner in the 7/7 inquests.

Lady Justice Hallett identified a series of inaccuracies in the information provided to the ISC for their investigation, arguing, "It is unfortunate, to say the least, that a body established by Parliament to review the work of the Security Service, in closed hearings, reported inaccurately in these regards and that these points were not corrected."[75] She also expressed concern about the quality of intelligence work being conducted in the identification of persons of interest and asked the agencies to "establish if there is room for further improvement in the recording of decisions relating to the assessment of targets."[76] These criticisms were echoed by the ISC in their annual report.[77] However, this was a rare example of bureaucratic processes being singled out as leading to poor operational performance. Such analysis would usually be conducted away from the public gaze in unpublished internal reviews.

Accountability mechanisms are also supposed to identify inefficiencies as well as ineffectiveness. In this regard, the ISC had a strong record of identifying problems, particularly prior to 2013, but struggled to effect change in policy or organizational direction. For years they expressed concern about the introduction of SCOPE II, a system designed to ensure secure messaging across a number of government departments, and stated that they were "appalled" that it was scrapped after tens of millions had been spent.[78] However, it was the Cabinet Office that had ultimate responsibility for IT strategy and so the extent to which the intelligence agencies were to blame is less certain.[79] The ISC repeatedly expressed concern over the lack of rigor in accounting for laptops and technical equipment that had gone missing, arguing "over a prolonged period, GCHQ has been unable to account for equipment worth up to £1M."[80] Four hundred and fifty of these pieces of equipment were believed to have posed a potential security risk.

Poor accounting among the intelligence and security agencies was a concern of the ISC from early in its existence, but became a prominent criticism over the last decade. Following a damning assessment of value for money in 2007, HM Treasury insisted that it would conduct six monthly assessments of the agencies from August 2008, including "examining progress on delivery of departmental strategic objectives, value for money, efficiencies, and financial management of the Single Intelligence Account."[81] In the ISC's Annual Report 2007–08, the director general of GCHQ said of the performance targets agreed upon with the Security Service: "We don't quite meet the targets they set, but, frankly, the targets they set out are at a level where it is very unlikely we would ever be able to meet them."[82] This statement did not attract any comment from the ISC, but it suggests a deeply problematic relationship between those setting targets and the agencies' ability or willingness to meet them. In 2012–13, the ISC described the performance targets set by HM Treasury in terms of eleven Agency Strategic Objectives (ASOs), including "counterterrorism, cybersecurity, counter-proliferation, counterespionage, supporting the Armed forces, and maintaining the ability to respond to events."[83] While they believed the agencies had performed well in their operational tasks, they identified "problems when working together on corporate issues," which were "in stark contrast to the Agencies' strengths when collaborating on operations."[84]

To some extent, the intelligence community faces a problem similar to that of other government departments whose role is to provide advice and analysis to government, such as the Foreign and Commonwealth Office, in that knowledge and understanding are not easily quantifiable. This makes setting precise targets difficult. However, these agencies are not beyond manipulating figures and targets for organizational gains. The ISC suggested that a "smoke and mirrors" approach to spending reviews had been adopted, along with "a tendency to claim savings benefits and efficiencies against rather intangible concepts, or by abandoning future projects that may have only been aspirational"—leading them to question how far real savings had been made.[85] Overall, one gets the sense from the reports that the intelligence machinery does make mistakes when it comes to some procurement programs and has flaws in its record-keeping, but performs at least as efficiently as other government departments.

Ethical Concerns

Since the agencies were put on a statutory footing, several examples of unethical behavior relating to intelligence have been brought to public attention. In the first place, there have been individual efforts to profit from selling state secrets, as in the 2010 case of Daniel Houghton, an SIS staff member who tried to "sell electronic files containing secret technical data and staff lists to a Dutch intelligence service."[86] Houghton pleaded guilty to two offenses under the Official Secrets Act and received a twelve-month prison sentence in September 2010. In 2001, a security guard working for Crusader at a BAE Systems site, was caught attempting to sell Russia details of new radar and electronic warfare systems connected to the Apache helicopter and Harrier jet. He was sentenced to eleven years in prison in 2002.[87] In each case, vetting and security systems were rechecked and SIS conducted a "lessons learned" exercise with regard to Houghton.

Periodic reports also emerge of individuals being investigated for selling secrets to foreign powers, but it is not clear what action followed from the original arrest. In September 2017, a "sixty-five-year-old woman" working as a contractor for an unspecified government department was detained under Section 1 of the Official Secrets Act, which relates to spying. The woman was apparently not working for the intelligence agencies but was arrested on the basis of an MI5 investigation.[88] As yet, no further information has been released about the investigation. In June 2018, a "man in his seventies," described as a "former Rolls-Royce employee," was questioned for allegedly plotting to pass secrets about the F-35 stealth fighter to China.[89] At the time of writing, no action had been made public, and the individual in question publicly denied the charges and protested their innocence. According to former security personnel, in other cases charges have not been pressed, provided the person in question cooperated and revealed the methods and motives of the foreign agents conducting the espionage.[90]

There have also been a number of instances where officials have been accused of negligence. In 2008, top secret government papers from the JIC were left on a train by Richard Jackson, a Ministry of Defence civil servant temporarily posted to the Cabinet Office. Jackson was prosecuted under the Official Secrets Act, pleaded guilty, and was fined as well as demoted.[91] There was also the case of an MI5 officer who had failed to declare that their partner was working as an escort, something that was revealed in the Max Mosley case in April 2008.[92] This prompted an internal review of vetting arrangements, and the individual resigned after being suspended. When the case was brought to public attention, officials emphasized that procedures were reviewed, but noted: "The process nevertheless relies on individuals being open and honest and informing the Service."[93]

This is a reminder that codes of conduct are necessarily a dialectic between the organization and its staff. Individual failings are inevitable in large organizations. What is most important is whether these are reducible in the future through better vetting, training, and tighter management. For this reason, the intelligence commissioner is said to have not been concerned with minor breaches of rules when they arose. Instead, overseers tend to look for "systemic sources of error."[94] If the system is arranged effectively, errors are outliers and individuals can be blamed. When they become closer to the norm, then the system needs changing.

The difficulty of such an approach lies in evaluating how far individual mistakes or instances of malpractice are symptomatic of wider problems. This became particularly apparent in the case of the mistreatment of detainees after 9/11. In its report on this issue in 2005, the Intelligence and Security Committee stated: "U.K. intelligence personnel conducted or witnessed more than 2,000 interviews in Afghanistan, Guantanamo Bay, and Iraq. Our investigations indicate that there were fewer than 15 occasions when there were actual or potential breaches of either U.K. policy or the international Conventions involving or reported by U.K. intelligence personnel. We have been told that there are no such incidents that have not been reported to us."[95] Specific examples were cited where individuals expressed concern over prisoner treatment, such as on January 10, 2002, when an SIS officer interviewing in Afghanistan reported on the handling of the detainee prior to the interview. The ISC stated, "the SIS officer in Afghanistan took no further action and the SIS informed us that while he remained in Afghanistan for a further three weeks, he did not witness any further instances of this kind. The SIS told us that they regarded this as an isolated incident."[96] The narrative put out by the agencies and accepted by the ISC was that these were individual cases and did not reflect any systemic position. ISC recommendations were notably mild and sought to correct rather than condemn inadequacies in training, communication with ministers, and legal advice and guidance.

This position was to change dramatically as a result of more rigorous investigation and public revelations. On July 6, 2010, David Cameron initiated an inquiry to "look at whether Britain was implicated in the improper treatment of detainees, held by other countries, that may have occurred in the aftermath of 9/11."[97] This was to be chaired by the Intelligence Services Commissioner Sir Peter Gibson. The rationale for the inquiry as set out by Cameron was that "for the past few years, the reputation of our security services has been overshadowed by allegations about their involvement in the treatment of detainees held by other countries," and that this was affecting public confidence as well as allowing "terrorists and extremists . . . to exploit those allegations for their own propaganda."[98] Thus it was designed to clear the air and provide a firmer understanding of what happened and what lessons could be learned for the future. The focus was only on the security and intelligence agencies and not the armed forces' use of detention.

From the outset, the Gibson inquiry was hampered by ongoing police investigations and court cases, which impeded its ability to scrutinize allegations. In addition, activist organizations, former detainees, and their representatives refused to cooperate due to concerns over the remit and the protocols in place to question witnesses and release information to the public. Nevertheless, thanks to internal reviews conducted by SIS and MI5 and other searches, the inquiry was able to compile a database of twenty thousand documents relating to detainees and identified "200 or so reported instances of the U.K.'s alleged involvement in, or awareness of, mistreatment of detainees."[99] It also noted inconsistencies over the reporting of suspected abuse, inadequate training, and variations between the written and oral guidance given to those sent out to question suspects. When it came to rendition, the written record produced by the agencies implied that guidance was issued on an ad hoc basis in February 2002, that "SIS could not actively participate in the rendition of foreign prisoners, and that this included arranging transportation or paying expenses." It also suggested that "SIS were not permitted to transport such prisoners to their native countries."[100] The overall impression was one of detachment from any policy of extraordinary rendition, which was depicted as a U.S. initiative.[101]

This narrative was severely undermined in 2011, when intelligence documents salvaged from the bombed-out headquarters of the Libyan External Security Organization suggested that U.K. personnel had cooperated with the rendition of a number of individuals to Libya in March 2004.[102] Specifically, Abdel Hakim Belhaj and Sami al-Saadi, their wives, and al-Saadi's four children. An SIS officer, Mark Allen, apparently communicated with the head of Libyan intelligence, Moussa Koussa, congratulating him on a detainee's safe arrival and noting, "This was the least we could do for you and for Libya to demonstrate the remarkable relationship we have built over recent years."[103] In asking for access to information from Belhaj, Allen gives a clear indication of the United Kingdom's contribution to the operation:

"The intelligence . . . was British. I know I did not pay for the air cargo. But I feel I have the right to deal with you direct on this."[104] The Gibson inquiry was suspended due to the police investigation that followed, and the ISC was tasked with taking up this issue in the future.

Allen was not prosecuted for this admission, in part because he had political authority from the Foreign Secretary Jack Straw. In a statement, Straw admitted, "On 1 March 2004, my approval was sought for some information to be shared with international partners. In almost every case such approvals were made by me in writing, on the basis of written submissions to me. However, in rare cases of great urgency, oral submissions could be made and oral approvals given by me. This is what happened on this occasion."[105] The U.K. government made a settlement with al-Saadi, paying him £2.2 million in 2012. In 2018, they made a settlement with Belhaj and his wife, Fatima Boudchar, which included a statement to the House of Commons, apologizing unreservedly and accepting that "The U.K. Government's actions contributed to your detention, rendition, and suffering. The U.K. Government shared information about you with its international partners. We should have done more to reduce the risk that you would be mistreated. We accept this was a failing on our part."[106]

The ISC's subsequent report, titled "Detainee Mistreatment and Rendition: 2001–2010," published in 2018, provided a far more rigorous investigation into U.K. involvement in these practices in the post 9/11 era than its earlier attempt. In terms of direct involvement, the report identified nine cases where verbal threats were made by officers during interrogation, thirteen incidents "where it appears that U.K. personnel witnessed at first hand a detainee being mistreated by others," and two cases in which "U.K. personnel were directly involved in detainee mistreatment administered by others." When it came to rendition, the report asserted: "The one aspect of U.K. policy which was clear was that the U.K. does not conduct rendition operations itself"; however, it concluded that its actions amounted to "simple outsourcing of action they knew they were not allowed to undertake themselves." For instance, it uncovered three individual cases where SIS or MI5 "made, or offered to make, a financial contribution to others to conduct a rendition operation," twenty-eight cases where the agencies "suggested, planned, or agreed to rendition operations proposed by others," twenty-two cases where they provided intelligence enabling a rendition operation, and twenty-three cases "where they failed to take action to prevent a rendition"—cases that included British nationals or residents.[107]

In the war on terror period, the U.K. government had repeatedly stated: "Our policy is not to participate in, solicit, encourage, or condone the use of torture or cruel, inhuman, or degrading treatment for any purpose."[108] A crucial aspect of this defense was that U.K. personnel on the ground, officials in Whitehall, and government ministers were not aware of mistreatment, and when they became aware, they took action to distance themselves.[109] Yet this notion was called into question by the ISC in the 2018 report, which alleged that it had "found 128 incidents recorded where Agency officers were told by foreign liaison services about instances of what appears to be detainee mistreatment."[110] Contrary to the narrative that instances of abuse were isolated cases, the ISC asserted they had found "38 cases in 2002 alone of officers witnessing or hearing about mistreatment."[111] The chief of SIS described these as "anomalies repeating themselves," but the report asked, "how many 'anomalies repeating themselves' it takes to realise that what you are seeing is not an anomaly."[112] Furthermore, once agencies became aware of mistreatment—or should have known, according to the ISC—they continued to supply questions or intelligence to liaison partners in connection with detainees being abused in 232 recorded cases.[113] In some examples, agencies were said to have developed a "work-around" involving "interviewing in a Portakabin just outside a detention facility," something the ISC said was "not an acceptable alternative to ceasing to engage with detainees being kept in unacceptable conditions."[114]

Thus, the ISC uncovered substantive evidence that U.K. personnel played a more significant role in detainee mistreatment and rendition than had been previously acknowledged. The U.K. government should also have been aware of the U.S. policy shift on torture after 9/11 much earlier than senior officials professed to be. As one commentator has suggested, not being aware "in itself points to an intelligence failure."[115] It is not as if there were not sufficient warnings given. In a three-hour briefing to senior MI6 officers on September 16, 2001, it is alleged that the then-head of the CIA's Counterterrorism Center, Cofer Black, gave what one attendant described as a "bloodcurdling" explanation of the United States' new approach, reportedly stating: "Our only concern is killing terrorists."[116] Attention was brought to this issue in 2002 via parliamentary questions.[117] Subsequent reports and investigations by various activist organizations and human rights bodies, as well as press reporting and leaks, highlighted practices of mistreatment and rendition before this was acknowledged by the intelligence agencies and guidance put in place.[118]

What the ISC could not identify was a coordinated policy to participate in or encourage torture or CIDT (cruel, inhuman, or degrading treatment). This conclusion is contrary to informed academic opinion, which asserts: "British intelligence and security agencies have worked hand-in-glove with counterterrorism partners to identify and apprehend suspects and disappear them into secret detention where torture was endemic."[119] The chief of SIS defended his organization against this notion, arguing: "We did thousands of detainee interviews. Set against this . . . the cases of concern are few."[120] Rather they represent the evidence as pointing to inconsistent practices and official guidance. Yet there was clearly an acquiescence to the risk of mistreatment, added to an unwillingness to acknowledge and condemn unethical practices. Although the ISC declared in relation to the Security Service, "It has been apparent in our dealings with the Service that there is generally a very strong sense of ethics, in addition to a keen observance of the law," they also noted that telegrams mentioning sleep deprivation were copied to multiple officers in early 2002 "none of whom remarked on the mistreatment."[121]

From this case emerge a number of issues, which are relevant when one considers intelligence accountability. The lack of ethical concern prior to legal guidance is arguably telling when it comes to weighing the relative importance of norms or laws in encouraging ethical behavior. Clearly, reporting to the ISC had been inadequate, and it took sixteen years before a detailed account of what had occurred could be presented. Even then, the ISC was forced to abandon its inquiry, as the government refused to allow them to interview the full range of participants from across all ranks of the agencies. For a decade after 9/11, the ISC was shown to be too ready to accept the accounts of the intelligence agencies and the government about their knowledge and involvement in torture and rendition. Meanwhile, it was activist groups, international human rights bodies, lawyers such as Clive Stafford-Smith, as well as tenacious journalism and academic scrutiny by individuals like Ruth Blakeley and Sam Raphael, that kept this issue alive and challenged the official narrative.[122] This suggests that a "clubbable" approach to accountability, whereby scrutiny bodies rely on the good faith of agencies to report information accurately, is not effective at gaining a full picture of intelligence practice.

Two other themes of ethical concern emerged in the past decade and attracted media commentary, namely: technology, including advances in surveillance capabilities and data capture, and the running of agents. With regard to the former, the revelations of Edward Snowden have provoked significant ethical debate over the role of intelligence in society and how it affects the relationship between governments and their citizens. In June 2013, Edward Snowden, a contractor working at the U.S. National Security Agency in Hawaii, downloaded up to 1.5 million data files before fleeing to Hong Kong. There he met with journalists Glenn Greenwald and Laura Poitras, to whom he gave thousands of classified documents.[123] This cache of information included a number of revelations about U.K. intelligence activity, such as that Britain had spied on delegates to the G20 conference in London in 2009, hacking phones and using an Internet café to obtain their passwords. It was also reported in *Der Spiegel* that the United Kingdom had launched a cyberattack on Belgacom, a partly state-owned Belgian telecommunications company in order to access smartphone users' data.[124] These revelations were embarrassing, since they seemed to violate norms of hospitality in the G20 case and of friendship in attacking a fellow European Union member state, Belgium.

More controversial domestically was the revelation that the United Kingdom was tapping into and storing "huge volumes of data" from transatlantic fiber-optic cables, which was then being analyzed for signs of criminal activity or security threats.[125] The United Kingdom apparently presented itself as having "a light oversight regime compared with the U.S." and its capacity to conduct bulk data capture led to it being labeled an "intelligence superpower."[126] This activity raised concern, as it seemed to lack targeting and in effect meant that the entire population's communications were being scrutinized—albeit at a meta level. A number of activist groups, including Amnesty International, Big Brother Watch, English PEN, and Open Rights Group, launched a legal challenge to this regime in 2013.[127] On September 13, 2018, they claimed a victory when the European Court of Human Rights ruled that historical mass surveillance programs breached the European Convention on Human Rights.[128] The court stipulated that a bulk interception regime "did not in and of itself violate the convention," but argued that the existing arrangements violated Article 8 (right to respect for private and family life) of the convention, as there was "insufficient oversight both of the selection of Internet bearers for interception and the filtering, search and selection of intercepted communications for examination, and the safeguards governing the selection of 'related communications data' for examination were inadequate."[129]

On the one hand, intelligence experts seem certain that mass interception is a vital tool in countering terrorism. As Mark Phythian puts it, "Collection needs to be undertaken broadly if it is to minimize the risk of missing anything that turns out to be significant."[130] Intercepting communications in real time rather than retrospectively means that potential security threats can be identified and prevented "upstream" in a way that minimizes the risk to public safety.[131] On the other hand, it also sets a precedent and framework for governments to be able to surveil their own citizens, which could enable political repression. Meta data includes information that could be used to identify individuals and learn private information about them—as evinced by the allegedly small number of people who have been fired for searching the datasets without authorization.[132] For this reason, a strong emphasis is placed on democratic safeguards and legal constraints. How far these are effective though is questionable. ISC members admitted that they knew of the surveillance programs revealed by Snowden, but did not seem to grasp the privacy issues raised. Some cabinet ministers in the coalition government suggested they either did not know about their existence or had only partial knowledge of their implications.[133] The government has argued that bulk interception and analysis is not intrusive if it is conducted by machines rather than humans, but this argument is rejected by privacy groups.[134] It is problematic, in part because the technology is designed and maintained by humans. As noted in chapter 1, algorithms and artificial intelligence systems can mirror the prejudices of their human creators.[135]

The issue of bulk data capture and analysis is an important one for both democratic accountability and competing notions of the public interest. While the ISC did produce a special report on the subject and made a major intellectual contribution to the subsequent Investigatory Powers Bill passed in 2016, this activity was only prompted by the Snowden revelations. It is legitimate to ask why the ISC had simply accepted the existence of these programs prior to the media controversy and not sought to bring them to public attention. In this regard, it seems they placed greater importance on maintaining secrecy and the confidence of the intelligence agencies than in ensuring the public were informed about what the agencies were doing. No doubt this would be defended on the grounds that revealing these programs might assist criminals and terrorists in avoiding surveillance, but the broad parameters of these activities could arguably have been noted, even if their technical operation remained secret. The public debate that followed Snowden, including reports by a number of prominent commentators and think tanks, demonstrated that it was possible to have an open and frank discussion about what kind of surveillance is appropriate and what safeguards are required. The ISC played an important role in this process, as when it corrected reporting that the United Kingdom was circumventing the warrant system by asking allies to conduct searches and then receiving the resulting intelligence via intelligence-sharing arrangements. Upon investigation, the ISC was able to support the agencies' claims that the allegations were groundless. However, the ISC had also failed to highlight a major shift in the scope and nature of intelligence gathering in the United Kingdom. In doing so, it underlined the importance of nonofficial sources of accountability, from media scrutiny to whistleblowing to public knowledge of intelligence activity.

A final set of ethical dilemmas has emerged in relation to agent-running. Three aspects to this activity have attracted press attention. In the first place, there are continuing investigations into the handling of agents in Northern Ireland during the Troubles. In particular, there is a live investigation currently underway by Bedfordshire Chief Constable Jon Boutcher, Operation Kenova, into how much police, army, and other government officials knew about or contributed to alleged murders, torture, and unlawful imprisonment associated with an IRA double agent code-named "Stakeknife."[136] This particular case highlights the practical and ethical challenges of running agents in criminal or terrorist organizations. Refusing to participate in criminal activity would risk exposing the agent's cover, but allowing them to commit crimes that cause harm to members of the public means that the government becomes complicit in that criminality. The seriousness of the allegations in the Northern Ireland context suggests this balance may not have been maintained in a number of cases.

The second concern over agent-running regards the behavior of undercover police officers, particularly where they developed romantic and physical relationships with individuals they were investigating. This attracted significant controversy when police officers infiltrating environmental activist groups were found to have engaged in intimate relationships and even fathered children with women who were unaware of their real identity. A serious problem over the consensual nature of these liaisons emerged, with one woman arguing: "If I had known that Boyling was a serving Metropolitan police officer—paid to deceive, control, and manipulate the environmental direct-action group of which I was part—I could never have consented to sexual intimacy with such an individual."[137] These cases did not directly involve personnel from the three main intelligence and security agencies, but serve to highlight some of the dilemmas that are faced in running agents at home and abroad.

Lastly, the use of child agents sparked controversy in July 2018, when a House of Lords committee revealed that the government was planning to increase the use of these sources. Again, this raises issues over consent, this time of the agents themselves, as well as concerns over the mental and physical welfare and safety of potentially vulnerable individuals.[138] In its March 2019 letter to Harriet Harman summarizing its findings, IPCO noted that since 2015, "17 CHIS authorisations relating to juveniles have been approved across 11 public authorities in total. Of the juveniles involved, one individual was 15 years old and all others were either 16 or 17."[139] IPCO suggests the practice is only used "in extreme circumstances" when "this option provides the best solution to breaking the cycle of crime and danger for that individual"; however, it is interesting that they also state: "in the vast majority of cases, this is only considered when the juvenile is already engaged in the relevant criminality or is a member of a criminal gang"—implying that in a minority of cases children are encouraged to join a gang or engage in criminality by public authorities despite not previously having done so.

Overall, the most serious ethical issues raised by accountability forums about the work of the intelligence and security services in the last two decades occurred during the initial stages of the war on terror period. The desire to assist the United States in its operations left the United Kingdom open to charges of complicity with torture and mistreatment of detainees overseas. A lack of training and official guidance, and poor reporting by the agencies, enabled this practice to continue for a number of years before media and academic scrutiny resulted in a fuller investigation that elicited a more complete picture of what had happened. In the same era, the United Kingdom assisted rendition operations on behalf of the Libyan government, despite denying its involvement in such activities.

To recap the above discussion, the existing systems of accountability have uncovered a number of failures by the national intelligence machinery. Political use of intelligence and oversight of the intelligence and security agencies has at times been flawed. When it comes to operational performance, it is apparent that the intelligence agencies are poor at predicting imminent changes to the security environment—reacting to threats as they arise rather than exercising foresight and aligning resources in anticipation of their emergence. They have also made errors on an individual and systemic basis, in relation to threat assessment and record-keeping in particular. With regard to ethics, the intelligence machinery was slow to appreciate and respond to the ethical dilemmas of the war on terror, the digital era, and the emergence of artificial intelligence. Many if not most of these problems have been highlighted by wider civil society first, and the formal scrutiny bodies have then reacted by pursuing investigations. It is clear that the latter alone are unable to either solicit accounts or hold intelligence and security personnel to account. Recommendations by the formal accountability mechanisms often seem to be ignored—as in criticisms of reporting or accounting of lost property, which were not acted upon. Accounts provided to these forums have been shown to be inaccurate, and personnel have hinted that deliberate efforts were made to conceal their activities from scrutiny bodies like the ISC. This exposes the limits of formal public accountability processes. They rely on the work of the media and civil society to provide an interactive mechanism for soliciting and checking the accounts of the intelligence and security agencies. Furthermore, most of the everyday activities of these organizations, their internal culture, and understanding of their role and constraints is not exposed to public scrutiny.

As such, the following chapters endeavor to contribute to the understanding of intelligence accountability by outlining how practitioners perceive it working in their day-to-day lives, both within the national context and in their interactions—liaison—with agencies from other countries.

THREE

Practitioner Views of Accountability

So far, the book has outlined the structure of formal accountability mechanisms in the U.K. intelligence community, set out how accountability is understood by commentators and theorists in public policy and intelligence studies, and then analyzed the main accountability issues raised by external commentary and oversight. This chapter examines the opinions of U.K. producers and consumers of intelligence, both serving and retired, as expressed in original interviews conducted for this project, bolstered by data from speeches, official documents, and public remarks. These individuals operate within the ring of secrecy in the United Kingdom, meaning they have firsthand experience of intelligence practice and the way accountability functions in this respect. The aim of this discussion is to see how far their personal understandings of the concept accord with theoretical and official frameworks. As will be seen in subsequent chapters, although formal external accountability structures are an important part of their conceptualization, when it comes to articulating examples of who gives and receives accounts, what factors provoke account-giving, and how officials are held accountable, intelligence practitioners also posit ad hoc, informal, and internal mechanisms as important.

In the first place, it is apparent that there are differences of opinion over the definition of accountability—and how accountability should operate. The idea of accountability as offering an account or narrative is evident in a number of responses. A former director general of the Security Service sees it as "the need to give an account of what you have been doing and to answer for the actions of the Service."[1] A former cabinet secretary avers that "what it means is that people should have to justify, to either internal or external scrutineers, what it is that they have done and validate their actions and conclusions in that way."[2] In both cases, accountability has two parts: one of explaining actions and the other of "justifying" or "validating" them. From that perspective, they mirror the dual understanding of accountability outlined in chapter 1 as being about both "rendering accounts" and an evaluative component of "holding to account."

Yet, among practitioners, there is a greater emphasis on accountability as about following the commands of elected leaders. As a former chair of the JIC puts it: "accountability for civil servants is to execute the instructions of a minister, or the government generally, to the best of your ability."[3] A former senior SIS officer concurs, arguing accountability is about "performing against the objectives that you are given and demonstrating an acceptable stewardship of state resources in doing that."[4] A former chief of SIS suggests that accountability "means that the actions and operations of the Service are carried out with the agreement of the government of the day and the Service is not acting independently."[5] However, there are subtle nuances between each position. In the first, it is clearly the government that is directing action; in the second, the intelligence community has to "perform" and "demonstrate" its "stewardship," opening up space for them to interpret government instructions (and reminding us that governments regularly change but the agencies abide in that stewarding role). The third quotation has government "agreeing" with the behavior—suggesting acquiescence on their part rather than strong central direction.

Interviewees present accountability in terms of discrete contexts and relationships. The chief of SIS cited above distinguishes accountability for the operations of the Service, what he terms "government accountability," from "parliamentary accountability." The latter involves overseeing "financial policy and administration" under the Intelligence Services Act, and they argue this cannot extend to operational matters: "You cannot have a system where Parliament is having oversight of operational activity. There is no explicit authorization process, nor should there be. It would be completely unworkable."[6] A former cabinet secretary presents a similar separation between "the validity of the assessment and the conclusions, which is the main subject of internal accountability" and "political accountability," defined as "the way in which these agencies operate because, by definition, they are intruding on other people's privacy."[7] In the context of the interview, the reference to "the way . . . these agencies operate" is given to mean broad policy direction rather than specific operations.

This understanding of the limits to accountability in operational terms is shared by members of the Intelligence and Security Committee, with one arguing:

> You cannot expect them to tell you who they might be giving twenty-four-hour surveillance, nor can you expect them to tell you how it is that they have managed to penetrate, either by human intelligence or by SIGINT, signals intelligence, the intelligence agency of another country, which has malign intentions toward the United Kingdom. You cannot expect them to be public to the extent that it undermines their ability to fulfil the obligation that is placed upon them.[8]

In practical terms, another member notes that "looking over their shoulders as they are doing whatever it is that they are doing" could adversely affect operations. Furthermore, in doing so "you would have the responsibility of knowing what was going on, but you would be powerless to influence it in any way."[9] For that reason, it is asserted that accountability has to be retrospective, with the oversight body maintaining a sense of distance.

The effect of this framing is to downgrade external accountability in favor of that which occurs within governmental structures. We can see this in the importance attached to ministers as the central locus of accountability. A former director of GCHQ asserts: "If the power of the state is being delegated through the secretary of state to an organization like GCHQ under the '94 Act, it follows that there has to be an accountability back upwards to the foreign secretary for the exercise of that authority. That is the basic model that GCHQ or any other government department would operate under."[10] A former national security advisor understands accountability first in the "classic British sense, namely that the intelligence community, like any other part of the public service, is accountable to ministers: ministers set the priorities and ministers are the customer that one is dealing with."[11] In relation to this, intelligence accountability is about "ensuring a good service to ministers with honesty and integrity."[12] There is an attempt by some respondents to define accountability in terms of this narrow relationship to the exclusion of wider sets of account-giving. For instance, as one interviewee puts it: "Accountability is indissolubly linked to authority in my mind . . . if you are providing someone with the authority to conduct a task, they have an accountability to you for the discharge of that task."[13] This echoes earlier definitions of accountability as about ensuring instructions are followed. A distinction is drawn between external bodies that provide "oversight" and internal mechanisms of accountability, meaning, for example, that "GCHQ is not accountable to the Intelligence and Security Committee in any meaningful sense of the word 'accountable.' "[14]

There is more to ministerial accountability than just the technocratic assessment of performance, however. The respondents denote three parts to this role, variously rendered as legal, moral, and political aspects,[15] or judgments about whether actions are "lawful, ethical, and appropriate."[16] Once these aspects are described, it becomes clear that they bring in a wider range of actors than the neat linear relationship between ministers and officials within agencies implied above. Legal accountability opens up space for lawyers and judges to give and receive accounts. Moral or ethical considerations play out in relation to public debates in wider society. Notions of appropriateness are defined by political networks and interagency cooperation, through which multiple organizational cultures affect decisionmaking. Even within any one agency, account-giving does not simply go up the chain of command but also laterally and diagonally to senior figures in other sections of government. For example, in relation to the appropriate use of resources, one interviewee notes "a kind of side loop of accountability if you are spending public money." In that context, "the personal authority of the accounting officer is therefore accountable to the Public Accounts Committee, not through the secretary of state."[17] This sets up a subdivision of accountability related to financial matters connecting civil servants with a different parliamentary select committee to the ISC. This conduit of accountability also flows through the post of national security advisor. As a former occupant of the role notes: "I would hold them to account about how they were spending their money. You know, they got significant amounts of additional money after 2010, particularly after the 2015 review. How are they spending that money and is it delivering results as intended?"[18] Thus, accountability operates across the machinery of government.

Moreover, officials note that existing legislation does not require them to consult ministers before undertaking operations. Rather, this is portrayed as "a practical mechanism that ensures that the intelligence services do not lose political support and political trust."[19] From that perspective, accountability by ministers can be either anticipatory or retrospective at the discretion of the agencies themselves. In practice, such autonomy is resisted. There is a firm sense that agencies would not launch operations without ministerial knowledge.[20] Ministers are viewed as very important, and civil servants perceive themselves as "only answerable at pleasure," meaning that they can be fired at the prime minister's discretion. Nevertheless, for this reason, civil servants can end up influencing ministerial accountability in turn. In order to "keep ministers warm," they may find themselves "looking after them when things are going wrong, giving them a way out in Parliament, what they should say and how to turn away tears and make it look like something else."[21]

This dynamic both reinforces the hierarchy of accountability—with officials reporting to ministers—and undermines it, since, in practice, ministers may become reliant on civil servants to provide the accounts they offer up to Parliament. The vertical hierarchy is also disrupted by horizontal political demands on ministers. As one former JIC chair relates it, "the accountability of a minister, obviously, is first of all to be loyal to their colleagues and to pursue an agreed policy and pursue it in a way which is obviously in line with the objectives of their policy."[22] This posits a horizontal accountability among cabinet and ministerial colleagues that is superordinate to the vertical framing that "they are, obviously, at the end, collectively accountable to the electorate."[23]

The respondents differ over how accountability to the electorate manifests itself. One former director of GCHQ stated: "GCHQ is not accountable to the media or to the public. It is accountable to the democratic representatives of the public if you believe in parliamentary democracy.

That is the basic structure."[24] However, one of their successors argued: "We have shifted from a situation where we only really needed to be accountable to the Parliament and the law to one where we actually have to be understood and accepted by the general public in a much more difficult environment to achieve that."[25] This is not seen as a wholly negative move, since many of the respondents felt that the general public were accepting of the role of the intelligence agencies and far less concerned about surveillance than civil liberties groups. To demonstrate this, one cited an editorial in the *Guardian* newspaper decrying the lack of outrage at the revelation of bulk data capture—with the implied reason being that the public supports that kind of activity.[26]

When it came to appraising the system of external accountability prior to 2013—in terms of the ISC, the intelligence services commissioner and surveillance commissioners, and the Investigatory Powers Tribunal—the interviewees were highly complementary. The ISC was widely seen as a useful body, since it acted as a conduit for the agencies to respond to negative reporting or allegations of wrongdoing. Indeed, this was a view shared by some ISC members, with one arguing "the biggest value of the ISC is to be able truthfully to give reassurance to society that wrongdoing is not being carried out by these agencies."[27] That is not to suggest the ISC was always expected to justify the actions of the intelligence and security agencies. Rather, the ISC was viewed as "an informed group who can criticize when necessary but also defend when necessary."[28] The ISC's members were perceived to be senior and discreet, and avoided the sort of grandstanding behavior associated with other select committees. This was attributed to the ISC's private nature, meaning "There was no incentive for people to say sort of eye-catching things just to get themselves on the telly, and I think that was of significant benefit to us. So, that helped to maintain the bipartisan style of the ISC and it also ensured that, actually, they were trying to understand rather than score silly points."[29] The commissioners, too, were apparently highly sympathetic to the role agencies played and the pressures they were under. Interviewees recalled receiving praise for the professionalism of their staff, with one commissioner apparently stating, "I have been very impressed by the way your staff take their responsibilities very seriously . . . they are not treating lightly the powers that they are exercising."[30] It is perhaps telling that few of the interviewees even mentioned the Investigatory Powers Tribunal, and those that did only referred to it in passing, with one stating it provided a "small degree of accountability."[31]

The overall impression conveyed is of external scrutiny bodies providing constructive and facilitative feedback rather than critical commentary on the agencies' work. Their existence is in itself supposed to act as a motivation to maintain standards, rather than any specific criticism made in overseers' reports. A former director of GCHQ describes this form of accountability as "like a shark net. Shark nets on beaches never actually keep sharks out . . . they sense, when they swim under a shark net, that they are trapped somehow, and they try and get back out again—immediately—rather than going and eating somebody. Well, it is a bit the same with the agencies."[32] This vivid description conveys an image of the oversight system as passive but still influential in deterring or correcting negative behavior. A number of respondents imply that this form of accountability is a positive process, whereas one that sought to be more intrusive would carry the risk of impeding operational effectiveness. Furthermore, accountability conducted via strict systems of control is conveyed as pointless, since "If the culture of the organization is wrong, accountability is always defeatable."[33] This is an interesting observation, as it reveals an ambiguity at the heart of representations of formal mechanisms of accountability. On the one hand, these processes are serious and important to agencies' understanding of their role; on the other hand, there are continual reminders of their limitations and weak links to everyday practice.

One is left to ask: how do the U.K. secret intelligence agencies maintain standards and perform to a high level (as they are generally perceived to) despite the limitations of external scrutiny? Beyond the formal mechanisms noted above, two processes are identified as important in the interviews. One is the nature of intelligence business and its continually evolving operational demands; the other is organizational culture, and specifically the internal mechanisms of account-giving and -receiving, which underpin the norms of intelligence practice. The first might be labeled "task-oriented accountability," the second "vernacular accountability." In the following sections, these will be outlined in more detail to provide a framework for the later chapters looking at U.K. intelligence accountability in practice in national and international contexts.

Task-Oriented Accountability

As noted in chapter 1, all bureaucracies risk atrophy if their activities are not open to public scrutiny. Intelligence practitioners refute the idea that this applies to them due to the dynamic nature of their tasks. Security threats are continually evolving, and this means that the intelligence organizations have to evolve in turn. This process is inductive and reactive—responding to external actions from opponents—rather than anticipatory and the result of a top-down managerial vision. The current director general of the Security Service argues: "What we have in the U.K. . . . was not designed and implemented in some giant leap . . . the U.K. has built and then advanced through many stages a set of defences over four decades in response to near-continuous severe terrorist threat . . . We have continually adapted, adjusted, and advanced what we do to counter it, applying hard-won lessons, sometimes painfully learned."[34] One of his predecessors compares the dynamic with that of wartime: "In the Security Service, we have got lots of baddies out there doing things and it is our job to stop them, and that means that you have a very acute, direct need to perform, because otherwise, you know, bombs will go off . . . It is a bit like when you go to war. You can get lots of things done, because everyone realizes there is a war on."[35] The strategic environment is framed as one in which opponents, whether they are terrorists, hostile states, or criminals, are constantly challenging the agencies. Thus, accountability is driven internally by the need to interpret and react to these external actors. As the speaker above suggests, "The drive to succeed and the fact that you have an active opponent trying to evade you helps to create a culture of 'How do we do that better and win next time?' "[36]

Adapting to new challenges also involves dialogue with new and old security partners internationally. In the post–Cold War era—as chapter 5 of this volume notes—the United Kingdom engaged in extensive dialogue with intelligence and security agencies in former Soviet states to compare techniques and processes of surveillance, intelligence-gathering, and analysis.[37] When it comes to relationships with key allies, especially the United States, there is a continual desire to demonstrate the United Kingdom's capabilities to ensure cooperation persists. The self-perception of practitioners is they are always looking to learn and develop rather than consolidate and preserve. While some comments imply mild tensions between the agencies, there is a general view that the national intelligence machinery focuses on efficacy more than turf wars or internal empire building.

Emphasizing operational effectiveness could carry the risk that officials would seek short-term gains, acting out of expediency rather than engaging in ethical reasoning; however, the sense from respondents, particularly those from the Security Service, is that this would undermine performance in the long run. Legitimacy is seen as such a vital part of intelligence work that having an ethical sensibility becomes an integral component of operational performance. One of the primary mechanisms for inculcating this is through training, which is conveyed as a rigorous process of interpreting past mistakes and learning for the future, allowing expanded dialogue and debate. An SIS officer recalls that for the training department, "cock-ups and horrors were meat and drink to them. You know, they were always on the lookout for training exercises that could be constructed on the back of egregious fuck-ups, so that they could provide your new intake with vicarious awareness of these risks and how to deal with them."[38] While errors may provoke defensive responses externally, internally the agencies clearly see them as an opportunity to improve performance. This is done via an extensive process of account-giving in the form of lessons-learned exercises and dissection of how particular behaviors led to negative outcomes.

The urgency of the task is also widely viewed as breaking down hierarchical barriers and encouraging a freer exchange of information than might be anticipated. An ethics counsellor for one of the agencies suggests that "hierarchy does not matter here. A relatively junior person would challenge a director if they thought they were right."[39] There is a continual emphasis on the flat structure of the bureaucracy, with few grades and high interaction between senior and junior staff—the better to increase communication about what works and what does not. This kind of fluid structure also serves to reduce the inhibiting effects of secrecy. Although the agencies have to maintain "Chinese walls" between them and their opponents, and between them and the public at large, to protect the informational advantage of intelligence, within the ring of secrecy there is a degree of candor and openness. A former SIS officer suggests: "Secrecy in any intelligence organization is never absolute, you always have to make pragmatic judgments, heuristics, about what can be revealed to whom and in what circumstances. You know, it is not something that remains static."[40] Thus, the extent and type of account-giving is shaped by the perceived demands of the task facing the agency.

In short, the nature of intelligence work, with its importance for national security and public safety, is seen as driving extensive reflection and learning, coupled with nonhierarchical and fluid systems of account-giving and -receiving. Intelligence professionals hold each other to account for errors, not because of fear of external oversight but because their sense of identity is inextricably bound up with the idea that they perform their tasks effectively. Nevertheless, there is the sense that, with some agencies, the overwhelming focus on the task could lead to negative behavior, at least in the short term. Where it demonstrably hampered performance or legitimacy, it would be likely to be picked up and corrected; but, if not, one wonders how often a system based on this kind of accountability would ask: Yes, it works, but should we be doing it?

Vernacular Accountability

As hinted at above, it is clear from the interviews that there is a wider system of account-giving and -receiving going on in the national intelligence machinery than just the formal institutional and/or legal mechanisms. In their day-to-day practice, intelligence officials continually interpret and communicate what they are doing and why, via dialogue and interactions with colleagues within the agencies, as well as peers across government and sister agencies abroad. We can term this "vernacular accountability," since it is a product of everyday conversations and experiences within the intelligence community. A senior SIS official notes: "One of the things you would do was regularly go and talk to new intakes and it was almost guaranteed that the first questions they would ask would be, 'Does the Service have boundaries? Where are they?' "[41] A number of respondents highlighted the questioning culture of their particular service and the extent to which officials offered accounts of their behavior to each other and solicited judgments about appropriateness. As an example, in the Security Service, it is argued that:

> The staff themselves would be shocked if we did something improper, and there is a natural reluctance on the part of the staff to push the boundaries. "Is it proper for . . . ?" They are always saying that. It is very much the culture of the organization. You know, "No, we can't. It wouldn't be proper to do that. It is disproportionate"; or, "I don't want to pursue this this way because it's too intrusive. Why can't we just do this?" That's sort of inculcated in people as they join, and it stays in the mind-set.[42]

The interviewee noted that some may be skeptical of this portrayal, but insisted it was an accurate representation of internal culture. It was also one repeated by others. Moreover, respondents offered additional illustrations of the abundance of account-giving in this field. A later director general of the Security Service noted that the staff counsellor is utilized by both lower level officials and senior management to offer accounts of behavior to a respected, quasi-external listener. Staff express concern about activities in a particular area and have the opportunity to "talk about it privately outside the management line," whereas management use the counsellor as a sounding board for new directions in policy, asking: "Does this sound right to you? Do you think we are going too far on this?" or "Do you see any angles on this that we ought to bear in mind from an ethics and accountability point of view?"[43] It is clear from this description that the staff counsellor is not just a means to launch formal complaints or air grievances but also someone that staff at all levels can contact to gauge appropriateness and turn to for ethical advice. In the context of the Security Service, the speaker implies that the question of "should we be doing this?" is regularly asked in conversations between colleagues, and in discussion with the staff counsellor, and this is a refrain across the intelligence machinery.

In addition to the staff counsellor, each of the three main intelligence agencies have ethics counsellors. These act as conduits for personnel who may be thinking, "I feel that something bad has happened and I want to blow the whistle," or for those who are unsure of the direction of policy and want to talk out their anxieties.[44] Beyond those immediate tasks, the ethics counsellors also see their role as fostering a critical and ethically aware environment. Their seniority varies according to the agency, but they operate independently of management and have significant status within each organization.

These kinds of formal procedures are further bolstered by more informal staff forums and chat rooms, allowing participants to raise issues anonymously or openly, depending on their preference, in a collective setting. Senior staff also indicated that their personnel could contact them directly: "My approach was to do a lot of walking around myself and make sure that people knew that the door was open and, if it wasn't my door or they didn't want to bother a director, then other directors in the management team were open to this kind of thing."[45] In other words, when it comes to deciding if actions are "lawful, ethical, and appropriate," the latter two are worked out through dialogue and reflection within the agencies and tested via consultative processes.

Vernacular accountability has its own specific constraints based on the seriousness of the task. In the first place, internal account-giving had to be honest. A former SIS officer notes: "There was tolerance of quite a lot of misbehavior in terms of sexual misdemeanors, but one thing that was totally out of court and beyond the pale was to lie to your colleagues. Once you had done that, there was no way back." This was because "if somebody had told you something about a case or an agent that turned out not to be true, and you made your assumptions on the basis of that untrue assertion, the consequences could potentially be catastrophic."[46] Thus, task-oriented accountability and vernacular accountability combine to enforce internal norms of truthfulness.

A second constraint of vernacular accountability is that account-giving has to remain internal. Whistleblowers who go outside official structures to air their concerns are discussed in highly negative and emotionally charged terms. It is a common assumption that "personal grudges motivate most whistleblowers,"[47] and they are framed as usually "deeply troubled individuals."[48] The emphasis is on the official system of counsellors, which "anybody of goodwill will use" and going to the media is viewed as "damaging and bad for the organization."[49] Indeed, vernacular accountability is conveyed as an antidote to whistleblowing. In the Security Service, it is argued that "virtually nobody ever went outside the Service to the whistle-blowing line, because these kinds of issues were debated openly within the Service."[50]

Those who have gone public are criticized for getting the facts wrong or refusing to acknowledge or investigate the context to the information they are revealing. This form of account-giving is also viewed as one-sided as, due to the need for secrecy, the intelligence agencies are not able to provide a full rebuttal to any allegations of wrongdoing. Recalling a negative experience of whistleblowing, a director general of the Security Service notes: "We were unable to answer that, because to say that that wasn't true, you would have to say what was, and then you would be compounding the damage."[51] Thus, secrecy is an impediment to a frank dialogue with the whistleblower. A contrast is drawn between secret organizations and public ones, in this regard. For the intelligence agencies, whistleblowing is seen as "orders of magnitude more serious and worse," because in "ordinary departments of government" the secrets that are being divulged will cause "embarrassment" rather than "jeopardize national security."[52] In other words, it is more likely that exposing an open organization's secrets will result in them giving an account in response, compared to a secret one, which might be inclined to close ranks to restore the integrity of that secrecy.[53]

From the above discussion, we can see accountability defined in different ways by practitioners. Some want to restrict it to formal reporting chains within an organization, going up to the minister responsible. Others include oversight bodies like the ISC and commissioners. Still others stretch accountability to the wider public and the media. (It is interesting that there is no suggestion that civil liberty groups should be offered accounts or incorporated into accountability forums. Rather organizations such as Liberty are generally framed as holding extreme views, which do not accord either with intelligence practice or the views of the public.) More recent practitioners tend to provide a more expansive definition of the term than their predecessors do. There is also some variation between agencies, with Security Service personnel stressing legal accountability and former members of the SIS downplaying this aspect—mirroring the level of legal scrutiny in the respective domestic and international contexts in which they mainly operate.

In discussions of how accountability works in everyday decisionmaking, the concept takes on a more fluid form and is conveyed as operating across organizational and even national boundaries. Here, the sense of accountability as about account-giving and -receiving is much stronger. What drives this process are two distinct but related aspects. One is linked to the task at hand, "task-oriented accountability," whereby the demands of countering the opposing actor compel officials to share accounts and interpret and respond to new developments. The other, "vernacular accountability," relates to the everyday deliberations between colleagues and partners, something very much shaped by the cultural norms and internal mechanisms for ethical debate of the U.K. national intelligence machinery.

Having set out how practitioners understand accountability, we now turn to exploring ways in which they perceive it to be changing. A number of processes have impacted on the way accountability is performed in the United Kingdom since the end of the Cold War. Five are given the most prominence by interviewees, namely avowal and oversight, the war on terror, the juridification of intelligence, social and cultural changes, and technological developments. These will be examined in turn to provide a sense of how wider political, social, and technological processes have influenced the formal structures of account-giving, the tasks intelligence professionals are seeking to fulfill, and the vernacular context to intelligence deliberations. The subsequent chapters go on to explore the relationship between these factors and the national and international practices of accountability.

Accountability in Context

One of the most significant changes to the status and practice of the intelligence agencies in recent decades was the decision to avow their existence and put them on a statutory footing in 1989 and 1994. This altered the relationship between Parliament, the public, and the intelligence community. The ISC's creation in 1994 empowered legislators to scrutinize intelligence in a way that was not possible before. One former director of the Security Service defines accountability as "being held responsible for what goes right and what goes wrong," something which is said to have "changed fundamentally with the passage of legislation."[54] The changes noted include more rigorous questioning of the agencies in the public domain, particularly by Parliament. As a former National Security advisor puts it, "I think, before that, parliamentary accountability was a little bit more self-controlled in the sense that prime ministers could go to Parliament when they felt they ought to go to Parliament, and it was difficult for Parliament as a whole to hold the government accountable for intelligence activity, because they were not aware of the intelligence activity."[55] Account-giving was extended not only to parliamentary committees. Once the Security Service was officially recognized, a former director general suggested it was "easier then to have a more open relationship with the world at large." This entailed making "a big effort to have journalists in and talk to them and try to get a better, more informed public discussion about what the Service was for and how it did its business."[56]

As such, the agency was offering an account to a wider circle of individuals beyond government and Parliament, although the content of this account was restricted to: "what we called in the Service 'the color of carpet question': we won't talk about operations, but you can ask anything else you like, including the color of the carpet!"[57] Such limitations would face continual challenge in subsequent years. One practitioner notes: "Once we opted, and it was we who opted, as I am sure you know, to go down the road of avowal and oversight, this brought in a necessarily wider concept of what accountability would be, because it is also, to some degree, accountability to the wider public and accountability to Parliament, which, up until that point, had been uninformed about and supremely unconcerned by these matters."[58] It is interesting that this person emphasized that the agencies themselves had called for greater openness and for being placed on a statutory footing—this idea was repeated by many of the practitioners interviewed but contradicted by at least one former member of the ISC. The reason the agencies were enthusiastic about legal status was that it imbued them with greater authority, both in terms of their self-identity and wider government structures. As a director general of the Security Service put it, this step "made us more operationally confident, because we knew we had the backing of the law and we knew we were able to handle that when it came to court and we were able to justify, or try to justify, what we were doing with the oversight mechanisms."[59] Similarly, a former chief of SIS argues: "It gave legal protection. It didn't inhibit operations; rather it renders actions legal, as they have been given clearance by the minister."[60] This underlines the point made in chapter 1, that accountability can have a positive effect on organizational morale and performance.

These legislative reforms were embedded during the 1990s, but the accountability mechanisms they established faced a particular set of challenges associated with the war on terror. A former diplomat and national security advisor argued: "The shock of 9/11 was so great, and the amount of money and resource that went into the intelligence agencies meant that the focus was on results, and maybe that mind-set about accountability was lost."[61] As was made apparent in chapter 2, the evidence does seem to bear this out in terms of the immediate aftermath of the attacks. In response to controversies over intelligence, the national intelligence machinery was restructured. With the creation of the national security advisor role in 2010, the scope to question civil servants on intelligence matters widened. A former advisor relays the changes thus: "As NSA, I was then subject to the oversight of the Joint Committee on National Security Strategy, with Margaret Beckett in the chair, and that was a more public kind of accountability. I had to get used to public hearings on intelligence, as that was the first time I had come across that . . . it is a relatively recent phenomenon, certainly, public oversight of civil servants in their use of intelligence."[62] Their successor saw the declining importance of accountability after 9/11 as having "since been reversed and now everyone is extremely aware of potential legal difficulties and obstacles and constraints."[63]

Thus, in addition to avowal and oversight, and the challenge of countering global terrorism, a third factor shaping intelligence accountability was the increasing influence of the law. For the security service, this process began prior to 9/11. A former director general traces the juridification of intelligence back to the 1990s, and "the appearance of our information, our intelligence, and our staff in criminal trials."[64] A key moment, according to this individual, was the Court of Appeal judgment in the Judith Ward case, stipulating that "all undisclosed, unused material must be disclosed."[65] This judgment was overturned in 1993,[66] but a lengthy legal discussion followed, with a number of test cases challenging when and how secret material, including intelligence, should be presented in court. In particular, once secret intelligence could be utilized in criminal trials, it created the problem of how that evidence might be scrutinized and tested. In 1997, the Special Immigration Appeals Commission Act was passed, which allowed hearings on immigration matters—such as deportations on national security grounds—to be held using closed procedures, with special advocates acting on behalf of the appellant. The same director general saw this as an important step for accountability: "That put into the witness box surveillance officers from the Service; desk officers from the Service; not very often, operational officers from the Service; and that is a form of accountability, a very tough form of accountability."[67] In other words, by compelling agents to give an account of their behavior in witness testimony, the law was facilitating new forms of account-giving, which were subject to challenge.

During the war on terror period, the government was regularly challenged over its use of secret intelligence in court proceedings related to detainees and those subject to control orders (later, "Terrorism Prevention and Investigation Measures," or TPIMS), which restricted their movements and activities such as Internet use. In response, the Justice and Security Act 2013 was passed, further expanding the opportunity for "closed material procedures" on national security–related cases. Special advocates with security clearance would again be able to interrogate the evidence against the claimant, but "cannot reveal precise details of the evidence and may only provide a 'gist' or loose summary." As such, it was reported that claimants "may not, therefore, be aware of all the allegations made against them."[68] The same year saw new guidelines allowing application for nondisclosure of evidential material if disclosure would present "a real risk of serious prejudice to an important public interest."[69] Account-giving was therefore being expanded, but within restricted parameters and only to legal representatives with security clearance.

Following the Edward Snowden revelations, the government acknowledged for the first time the extent of government capture and surveillance of communications, and the Investigatory Powers Act 2016 established a clearer legal framework for this activity. The result, as an intelligence consumer puts it, is that "the controls on the agencies in terms of the legality of what they do, the proportionality of what they do, are far tighter than they used to be twenty or thirty years ago. You know, they have judicial commissioners, the warrants need to be signed, the commissioner scrutinizes, and the ISC can control, and the whole process is tighter and more demanding. There is far more legal input into intelligence work these days."[70] Yet such scrutiny operates within limits. In particular, the challenges of communicating how the intelligence agencies are using technology, and the implications of that work, are difficult for nonexperts in parliamentary committees or the judiciary to understand. A current practitioner notes: "You can't necessarily easily explain to a judge the intricacies of a neural network."[71] That suggests that some aspects of operational activity do not lend themselves to account-giving outside the agencies themselves—unless the audience is subject to secrecy constraints and is an expert in a relevant field.

A fourth process affecting intelligence organizations is the substantive social and cultural changes that have taken place in wider British society, both since the 1960s and accelerated after the Cold War. These had an effect on the kinds of people that work in the field, their attitudes with regard to secrecy and intelligence, and the views of the wider public toward intelligence practice. Staff recruited in the 1970s recall that the agencies were dominated by male ex-colonial civil servants, some of whom had held senior posts in Africa, Cyprus, Malaya, and other locations in the empire before ending up in MI5 after independence.[72] Although often fascinated by other cultures and retaining links with friends around the world, they also expressed themselves using the racial epithets of the day and "went off the boil after lunch"—implying their work rate declined after eating and drinking at midday.[73] Domestically, the Security Service was seen as "a pretty ropey outfit," and when it came to SIS, there were widespread references to liaison agencies using torture to obtain information from detainees. A generational shift is identified, with graduate recruitment and, in particular, an increase in female officers in operational roles transforming the working environment. In the Security Service, reform was further advanced by the appointment of an outsider, Anthony Duff, as director general, following the scandal of an MI5 officer, Michael Bettaney, passing secrets to the Soviet embassy in London. Duff is said to have appointed a director to manage reform, resulting in "new procedures, new staff arrangements, new grading system, different recruitment." Overall, a more "work-orientated" approach was instituted along with a change in direction away from subversion and toward counterterrorism.[74] At the same time, intelligence came to be seen as a public good, and the focus was increasingly on protecting individual citizens rather than the collective.[75]

Further changes occurred in the 1990s, with the wider acceptance of LGBTQ individuals in sensitive posts. In a recent speech, Robert Hannigan, director of GCHQ, contrasted the treatment of "Ian," a member of staff in the 1960s, who was "interrogated on suspicion of being homosexual . . . summarily dismissed, and escorted out of the building," with "Emma," a current cyber-defense analyst, who used a staff blog to announce her transition and received the following reaction: "Not only was it the most 'liked' blog we've ever had, the comments were incredibly supportive: genuinely fascinated . . . full of respect and admiration, and sincerely wishing her well on the difficult path she described so well."[76] This example underlines the importance of vernacular accountability, with colleagues reinforcing the acceptance of diversity—in a different direction from that of the previous generation, which used racist terminology and shared stories of mistreatment by liaison agencies, projecting a more reactionary image of intelligence practice.

In the contemporary era, younger members of intelligence organizations are said to diverge further from their predecessors when it comes to deference to authority and willingness to dissent from official policy. As one practitioner put it: "There is a generational shift. Young people now are used to being listened to and expressing their opinion. If somebody felt their concerns were not listened to, they would say so."[77] In that sense, they are depicted as being less accepting of official narratives and more likely to question and offer alternative accounts of appropriate behavior. Yet, in some ways, speakers see the new generation as more acquiescent, particularly when it comes to governmental and corporate intrusion into their privacy. One former practitioner avers that "most of the British public don't really care that much."[78] Another argues: "I actually don't believe that the under-thirties, or even the under-forties, these days place the sort of value on privacy that earlier generations—or *Guardian* readers among earlier generations—did. It's just they freely expose themselves in fora which they don't consider in the least secure." Indeed, this individual believes that for this reason, "the whole business of accountability has been totally transformed by social media."[79]

This leads us to the fifth development affecting the accountability context: technological change. Since the digital revolution, the intelligence and security services have rapidly expanded their capabilities to harness and analyze data. These resources have been used extensively to identify and neutralize threats from transnational criminals and terrorists. In the process, a much wider range of people have become subject to intelligence interest and surveillance. Among practitioners, this capacity is represented in highly positive terms; however, it is accepted that the systems in place to conduct this kind of intelligence work are highly complex, and this in itself can create problems for ensuring that producers and consumers are sufficiently informed about their operation to provide consent and monitor their use. On the one hand, it is noted that many aspects of this technology are already affecting our day-to-day lives: "Pretty much everyone has AI making decisions for them all the time already. For instance, the firewall on your phone decides what gets through and what doesn't."[80] On the other hand, the growth of this kind of activity and its potential utility mean that "we also have a moral duty to society to explain how it works."[81] The novelty of this challenge is such that only the currently serving officials acknowledged this as a transformative issue for accountability. Nevertheless, when prompted, a number of respondents noted that this was a challenge for intelligence practitioners, although it was seen as something affecting society at large.[82]

To summarize, practitioners tend to define intelligence accountability in terms of formal lines of delegated authority and following instructions. Scrutiny bodies do affect behavior, but usually in a more diffuse way, through their very existence rather than via specific actions undertaken or recommendations made. Importantly, these accountability mechanisms are only one part of a wider system of accountability, which includes self-correction, organizational learning, and interactive interpretations of appropriateness between officials and other private and public actors. Two other key factors serve to keep these organizations honest and drive innovation. These are the task at hand (here, labeled task-oriented accountability) and the internal culture and everyday interactions between practitioners (here defined as vernacular accountability). While the formal structures of accountability have been tightened over the last two decades and legal aspects have become especially prominent, task-oriented accountability and vernacular accountability have also been enhanced. Social and cultural changes in wider society have infiltrated the agencies and meant that a more professional approach to intelligence work has been adopted. In addition, technological enhancements have led to exponential growth in the capability and efficiency of the intelligence and security services—making them more effective at performing their tasks, even as their opponents have become more challenging thanks to their access to disruptive technologies.

Meanwhile, avowal and the freer exchange of information across the national intelligence machinery mean that more fruitful and pervasive conversations about intelligence practices are now available than in the past. As chapter 4 will describe, vernacular accountability has flourished in an era when online platforms and secure digital communications allow anonymous ethical discussion—especially when combined with wider dialogues between industry, activists, and other agencies at home and abroad. And as I discuss in the conclusion, this could be extended to allow greater public participation in intelligence policymaking.

FOUR

National Intelligence Accountability

The previous chapter explored how members of the national intelligence machinery and their overseers understand the concept of accountability and how they perceive its milieu changing in recent decades. This chapter builds on that description, going into more detail on how accountability works in practice in the U.K. context. Three mechanisms were identified above as salient, namely: (1) formal structures of reporting (including ministerial authority, legal rules and constraints, and oversight from the ISC and IPCO); (2) operational demands, or "task-oriented accountability," whereby changes to the threat environment, new technologies, or government priorities compel reflection on what works and what does not; and (3) vernacular accountability—the everyday interpretative effort made by intelligence practitioners to ensure their activities fit with the culture of their organization, the norms of wider society, and the expectations of customers at home and abroad. By examining public statements of intelligence consumers and producers, bolstered by interviews with former and current intelligence practitioners, this chapter aims to see how far practice aligns with theoretical understanding, as well as consider which of these modes of accountability is more important in shaping behavior.

As noted in chapter 3, a primary locus of accountability identified by interviewees is the government minister; however, their status within the formal structures of accountability is ambiguous. On the one hand, they will approve operational decisions and thereby endow them with political authority; on the other hand, the civil servant who heads the agency is the legally responsible individual, and the initiative for warrants and other investigative actions comes from the services.[1] Nevertheless, ministers are clearly a central focus for the construction and dissemination of accounts of intelligence behavior. Prior to seeking ministerial authorization, an extensive process of discussion and revision of submissions takes place within the agencies themselves. As a former senior SIS officer puts it:

> It was clearly in nobody's interests to send across a stream of flaky, ill-thought-out and tenuous submissions that would not command confidence. So, there was an element of self-censorship here . . . senior operational officers would normally look at these things quite carefully from that perspective. And then, there was an SIS secretariat that would look at them and, often, you would get them sent back: "We're not sure about this. Could you clarify X or Y?" So, within the organization, there was this process. Then, it would be sent to the relevant FCO director or director general, and he or she would look at it and might well have views about whether this is something, in their judgment, that the foreign secretary would not be happy about, or would be happy about, or would not understand, or "Could you clarify this, that, or the other? And, when you say that this is legal, we want our legal advisors to take a view," that sort of thing.[2]

The level of bureaucratic scrutiny here is striking, with multiple levels of assessment of the clarity, accuracy, and validity of the application, encompassing consultation with the FCO and legal advisors. With a wider net of individuals contributing, intelligence submissions could be very lengthy—over twelve pages, compared to the normal three to four pages for a standard policy submission.[3] A number of interviewees expressed surprise at the size and detail within submissions, with a former cabinet secretary stating, "I always wondered how it was that the home secretary and foreign secretary ever found time to do anything else."[4] William Hague, when he was foreign secretary, offered a glimpse of the volume and nature of this activity from the ministerial perspective:

> I see operational proposals from the Agencies every day, amounting to hundreds every year. The proposals are detailed. They set out the planned operation, the potential risks, and the likely benefits of the information to be gained. They include substantial legal sections, which set out the basis for the operation and comments from senior Foreign Office officials and lawyers.[5]

Hague notes that he would discuss submissions with officials from other agencies and colleagues, particularly the home secretary, and scrutinize them carefully before a judgment was given in response. Such deliberations combine elements of formal accountability, in terms of officials reporting to a senior point of contact, then the warrant-granting department, leading up to ministerial authorization;[6] task-oriented accountability, involving a judgment about whether the operation would be likely to achieve its goals; and vernacular accountability, with individuals at various levels debating their peers about appropriateness. As such, formal written submissions clearly entail a dense pattern of account-giving and -receiving.

On this evidence, it is apparent that submissions garner serious attention. A former minister and later member of the ISC implied that self-interest was driving this: "I think you always try to be meticulous . . . my feeling is that most ministers will do that because, even if they are not that ethical about it, they know that, at some point, they might have to account for what they have done before Parliament."[7] Similarly, a director of GCHQ described the minister as "the owner of our political risk," and so would always be thinking, "If this leaks out, am I prepared to defend it?"[8] Thus, retrospective accountability to Parliament (and an implied accountability to the media or general public) clearly features in the mental calculations of ministers authorizing operations.

In addition to concern about parliamentary scrutiny, the legal ramifications were also borne in mind. One official suggested, "Extreme care went into making sure that there were no legal risks."[9] This is a response to perceived failures in the past, such as Iraq. In the current climate, it is argued, "The heads of intelligence agencies are very, very aware of the risks that they and their officers face legally and are therefore desperate to dot the i's and cross the t's in advance to make sure they have full legal cover."[10] In practice, that means the minister must approve actions, and so they, in turn, will want to ensure they are not exposed to future legal action. According to Hague, submissions are judged on the basis of necessity, proportionality, and the level of targeting—in line with legal requirements, as well as a political judgment about how far the infringement of an individual's privacy is justified for public safety or national security reasons.[11] The ordering of these considerations is perhaps relevant, implying legal aspects are covered first, followed by ethical or political questions.

Some interviewees hinted that the level of scrutiny would vary between ministers, based on the personalities and interests of the individual in question. A former national security advisor asserts: "Some would no doubt read them extremely carefully, ask questions, and push back, and some would just tick them off and say, 'Yeah, get on with it.' It just depends entirely on the foreign secretary or the home secretary."[12] One of their predecessors suggested that the institutional position of the individual is also important:

> The home secretary is very involved in the warrantry of the Security Service, because a lot of it is not just sort of consuming finished intelligence, it is authorizing the myriad of activities. So, the home secretary is signing warrants all the time and is very close to the Security Service process. The foreign secretary is still close to what SIS are doing, but perhaps a bit less close to it. And, of course, the prime minister doesn't sign warrants and isn't involved in authorizing, so is one step back again, and different prime ministers will take different levels of interest in it.[13]

From this description, the home secretary has more involvement in the Security Service's operational processes than the foreign secretary would have with SIS, and the lack of institutional base for the prime minister means they lack day-to-day contact with officials about operations. In other words, there is a real variation in the density of account-giving and -receiving, depending on the service. This makes sense when you consider that the vast majority of warrant applications (which have formalized accountability rituals via the authorization process set out above) come from the Security Service.

The level of scrutiny also differs according to the type and timing of submission. The above process relates to formal written submissions, but ministers approve operations in a more ad hoc manner at times. A former intelligence officer notes: "There were occasions when we would have to get somebody out of bed at three o'clock in the morning and say, 'Can we do this now, please?' Occasionally, you would do things orally, written submission to follow."[14] This is necessary at times due to operational pressures, but means the minister has a less substantial basis on which to judge the appropriateness and wisdom of the proposal. The scope for this kind of request inevitably opens up the possibility of officials using it to circumvent normal reporting processes to railroad a minister into approving action. Whether this occurred in relation to the Libyan rendition case, it is notable that it was verbal approval that was obtained from Jack Straw in the first place, at least according to him. Furthermore, in its first report, IPCO criticized the retrospective paperwork for these approvals, implying it used "boilerplate text" and "standardized wording that can obscure the precise limits of their knowledge."[15]

Since they do not generally originate requests for action, the key power of ministers lies in their capacity to veto or amend submissions. Secrecy prevents an accurate estimate of how many submissions are approved by whom, but Hague repeatedly emphasized that he did not approve all requests.[16] Most respondents indicated that ministers refused applications at times—with the tenor of commentary suggesting this was normally due to legal or political risks being seen as too high. The most recent data indicates 1.71 percent of requests were declined by the "designated person" responsible for authorizing requests, a category that includes ministers.[17]

Beyond the authorization process, some officials indicated that ministerial oversight was limited. Again, this depended on the agency. In particular, the relationship between the foreign secretary and GCHQ seemed to be more distant than ministers and their departments in other parts of the national intelligence machinery. As a former director put it, "I had to get the secretary of state to fight for my budget, which he did; but if he was going to do so, he had very little choice but to present it in the terms that I put to him. That was because he did not have enough transparency into the organization and was not the primary consumer of its intelligence."[18] This could also be due to the complex and technical nature of GCHQ's work, and is not necessarily true of all intelligence and security services. Nor is it the case that ministers are passive in their receipt of information.

Rather, it is argued that "the intelligence agencies have got weekly contact with ministers, who are probably asking them detailed questions, specific questions, maybe different questions, which they then have to feed into their tasking."[19] According to this framing, the operational activity of these organizations is continually shaped by ministerial inquisition. What the quotation from a former director of GCHQ highlights is that ministers are ultimately reliant on the good faith of officials to provide accurate and sufficient accounts about secret activities.

Overall, we can see that the desire for ministerial authorization provokes a series of account-giving processes between the agency and the minister, between the minister and officials, and between the minister and their colleagues. Although the scope exists for officials to operate independently of the minister, in practice the agencies are keen to ensure they have the political and legal cover that ministerial authorization affords. A former security minister records their impression of the agencies as being "so conscious of the suspicion that intentionally surrounds their actions that they are ultra-cautious" and so tend to say, "No, we will refer upwards rather than do something that's borderline."[20]

Aside from their relationships to ministers, the agencies also have formal reporting requirements to other organs of government, notably the National Security Council and the national security advisor. A former occupant of the role defined themselves as "line manager for the heads of the intelligence agencies and a key link between the production community and ministers as the main customers."[21] In practice, as one of their successors put it, this meant the agencies were given a single departmental plan, and every quarter their heads were invited to attend a meeting and asked, "What have you achieved over the last three months against your objectives?"[22] Since the inception of this position, the national security advisor has played a pivotal role in mediating between the intelligence and policy worlds, soliciting accounts from the agencies about their work and transmitting the priorities of the government in return. How far this office will continue to function in that manner is currently open to question, since it was announced in February 2019 that it would be permanently merged with that of cabinet secretary, who is also head of the U.K. civil service. It is hard to see how one individual could play such a hands-on role in coordinating the national intelligence machinery and holding it to account along with the extensive commitments of running the civil service as a whole and coordinating with the cabinet—as a number of former practitioners pointed out at the time.[23] Nevertheless, the post continues to exist and is supposed to function as before.

The National Security Council's framework for tasking the agencies emerges from an annual review by the Joint Intelligence Committee, setting out the requirements and priorities for secret intelligence, ranked according to three orders of importance. (British intelligence officials do enjoy ranking things into three categories. The JIC ranks intelligence assessments in terms of best-case scenario, middle-case scenario, and worst-case scenario; intelligence assessments are also rated in terms of high confidence, medium confidence, and low confidence.)[24] Agencies will offer accounts in these forums, since their heads are also members of the JIC and attend the NSC when required. Yet it is questionable how far they perceive themselves as accountable to the NSC or the NSA. In their rare public speeches, neither the chief of SIS nor the director general of the Security Service even mention them.[25] For Alex Younger, it is the "double-lock of Ministerial and Independent judicial authorisation" that means "MI6 is accountable and so is every single officer who works here."[26]

As discussed earlier, the passing of the Investigatory Powers Act in 2016 meant that judicial commissioners are now involved in approving warrants and can access and review records. It is clear that this is seen as a major development in the formal accountability processes of the intelligence machinery. A former national security advisor indicates that the presence of judicial commissioners approving warrants, combined with the work of the ISC, mean that "the controls on the agencies in terms of the legality of what they do, the proportionality of what they do, are far tighter than they used to be twenty or thirty years ago . . . There is far more legal input into intelligence work these days to make sure it does pass all those tests."[27] A former member of the ISC sees internal scrutiny by commissioners as "more important" even than the work of the ISC, "particularly when that bolsters the decisions of the home secretary and foreign secretary giving warrants, I think that's more important."[28]

The Investigatory Powers Commissioner's Office (IPCO) has extensive powers to scrutinize warrant authorization as well as the training, security governance, network access controls, auditing, and other aspects of the management of information acquired through investigations.[29] The commissioner's office is in its infancy, and the scope of its mandate is still being worked out through negotiation with the government and the various public authorities it holds to account. However, it is worth noting that its scrutiny of warrants and operations relates primarily to activities within the United Kingdom. By contrast, the IP commissioner acknowledges that, overseas, class authorizations mean there is much less detailed information on individual actions, and judicial commissioners do not have a role in approval. IPCO staff see themselves as operating within well-defined limits: "We don't have oversight of general agency work that does not come from the use of investigatory powers—unless we receive a specific direction from the prime minister."[30] The primary concern for IPCO is when operations may partially entail activity in the United Kingdom, or where a U.K.-based individual is involved, as these fall under the scope of the RIPA—or where intelligence is likely to be used in a U.K. court. Moreover, the "Overseas Security and Justice Assistance (OSJA) process," whereby "public authorities assess the Human Rights and other implications of cooperative relationships with organizations in other countries," currently falls outside their mandate—which the commissioner argued was inconsistent with their purpose.[31] This suggests a distinct separation between the domestic accountability regime and that which operates abroad.

The commissioner did request and receive several briefings about SIS's overseas agent-running, or "Covert Human Intelligence Source (CHIS)" activities.[32] They also conducted two inspections of SIS's overseas stations in 2017 and separate inspections of the FCO's work with SIS and GCHQ.[33] During the course of these, inspectors questioned individuals about how systems worked in practice. In this way, the IP commissioner was able to solicit accounts from officials at a range of levels within the intelligence agencies and the FCO, and gauge the culture of these organizations. As one of IPCO's inspectors puts it: "We try and test their cultures, as you would expect, around how forward-leaning they are, how focused they are on compliance, necessity, proportionality, and collateral intrusion."[34] Furthermore, this is seen as welcomed by the agencies themselves: "There is a measure of reassurance for them if they've got that right and equally; if they haven't, they are prepared to learn from it, and the only way they can do that is by us looking at them."[35] IPCO interacts with the agencies on an almost weekly basis and there is extensive ongoing dialogue, although formal inspections are signposted well in advance and generally occur at regular intervals.

Overall, IPCO's use of inspections, as well as the role of its judicial commissioners in approving domestic warrants, gives the sense that it does dig deeper into operational practice than previous accountability regimes. That said, the fact that its oversight domain extends to all local authorities in England, Scotland, and Wales, as well as all the law enforcement and intelligence and security agencies, means that its capacity is stretched. In total, IPCO is responsible for inspecting over 600 organizations. It conducted 59 inspections of law enforcement agencies in 2017, 134 at local authorities, and 21 at other public authorities, in addition to the biannual inspections at each of the three intelligence and security agencies.[36] In light of the demands on their time, the commissioner expressed a desire to monitor staffing and resource levels to ensure they could carry out their mandate.[37]

The role of the ISC has been revised substantially in recent years, but there is a similar ambiguity about the full extent of its powers and remit to investigate operational matters. There is general agreement that the ISC has acquired more powers and now has more impact in terms of its influence on intelligence policy. This is, in part, the result of legislative changes, but also linked to personnel changes. One commentator argues that the ISC tends to "take on the persona of the chair," and the prior experience of the current incumbent, Dominic Grieve, as attorney general is said to have led him to want to get more involved in operational aspects—leading to tension with the agencies.[38] The increase in criticisms of the intelligence machinery within recent ISC reports has compelled these organizations to be more responsive and redressed the previous sense of the ISC as overly passive in its questioning. Given that the ISC's chair is to be afforded an official role as the ultimate external conduit for whistleblowing for intelligence personnel, this could become a more contentious position in the future. Yet one of the prime assets of that committee often cited is its lack of political agenda and discretion. If it continues to adopt a more public-facing, and publicly critical, stance, and the chair's role becomes politicized, then a number of interviewees implied there is a risk that the ISC will no longer enjoy the confidence of the intelligence and security agencies.

Curiously, the most significant dispute in the ISC's history has been with the government, rather than with the agencies. In November 2019, Grieve accused the prime minister of delaying, for political reasons, an ISC report into Russia's interference in elections, espionage, and subversive activities. The delay was presented by the government as a normal process of checking and redacting, but Grieve refuted that suggestion: "What Number 10, the press office, or whoever the spokesman has said is completely and totally untrue. It's a lie. . . . The process of getting this report cleared is finished. The last stage, the clearance by the prime minister, is programmed for ten days."[39] A government spokesperson implied that committee members had leaked the report's contents and the exchange became personalized, with Grieve questioning the prime minister's fitness for office. It is possible to see this as simply a dispute between Grieve and the prime minister, as the former had been a prominent opponent of Boris Johnson's handling of Brexit. However, in a parliamentary discussion on the report, a succession of former and current ISC members disputed the government's account and argued for the report's release. For Grieve, the government's refusal to release the report "called into doubt the point of having an Intelligence and Security Committee at all," and he argued for changes to the system to remove the prime minister's ability to delay.[40] Importantly, he grounded his arguments in the public interest and the importance of keeping them informed—underlining how far the ISC's emphasis had moved under his direction.

As noted in earlier chapters, the Treasury has an important role in scrutinizing the activities of the national intelligence machinery, along with the National Audit Office. Although intelligence officials have admitted they do not meet the targets the Treasury sets, the regular assessments conducted after 2008 involved substantive investigations into the efficiency of these organizations. The impression given by agency heads is that the Treasury and the NAO have a deeper understanding of the performance of the intelligence agencies than the minister responsible—at least in efficiency terms. Such an appraisal is still limited, however, since intelligence activity is resistant to quantification. This is conveyed by a former SIS officer's remark: "When I started engaging with the Treasury on these issues around the turn of the millennium, they started off trying to adopt a very narrow, mechanistic approach, on the number of reports produced, and I said, 'Well, that's basically damn right silly, because it creates a perverse incentive to take one report and split it into six small ones . . . so I think we need to be a bit more sophisticated than that.' "[41] Intelligence work has a high degree of latency by its very nature. It takes time to build up an intelligence picture of a security threat, develop a human contact who might become an agent, or collect and analyze large data sets for items of national security interest. With the increase in available information in the digital era, there is a greater amount of redundant effort being undertaken to sift through irrelevant material. Much of this can be done via computer systems, but the human intelligence aspects still require time and effort to foster. As a result, the process whereby intelligence agencies report to the Treasury is problematic when it comes to evaluating their efficiency, since knowledge and understanding are resistant to quantification, and outcomes are not easily traced back to intelligence in a simple linear fashion.

That said, practitioners acknowledge that more could be done to improve the managerial efficiency of their organizations. For one thing, the intelligence agencies receive their government funding via a single intelligence account. That means that the individual spending of each organization is conflated into one budget—reducing the incentive for any one of them to introduce dramatic reforms in the name of efficiency. Even if they did want to make changes, the second challenge is sourcing useful recommendations. A number of interviewees expressed skepticism over how far the ISC was able to offer constructive advice or criticism when it came to running an organization more efficiently—given that it is made up of parliamentarians rather than management experts.

Thus far, it has been shown that the formal reporting aspects of accountability are taken seriously by practitioners but come with an inherent set of limitations. Officials acknowledge that ministers do not have a full picture of the efficiency of their organizations. Ministers are perceived to scrutinize operational requests carefully, but on occasion they are asked for verbal agreement without the extensive evidence base of a written submission. The strongest element of accountability via formal reporting identified by interviewees came with the introduction of judicial commissioners. Their involvement in actual operational decisions is seen as the most intrusive mechanism for soliciting and appraising the accounts of officials. This is followed by ministerial authorization and Treasury analysis of performance targets. Oversight bodies, such as the ISC and commissioners, contributed to the sense that the agencies were being scrutinized, but were either conveyed as sympathetic and pliant or as necessarily distant from the day-to-day practice of intelligence work. Meanwhile, the Investigatory Powers Tribunal was not discussed in any depth, and no examples of its activity or findings were raised in the interviews.

In isolation, many of these accountability elements may seem inadequate, but they are often grouped together in the rhetoric of officials as a connected system of formal reporting requirements that add up to more than the sum of their parts. Indeed, one official compares the accountability of intelligence agencies favorably with other organs of government: "Government departments are not subject to virtually any scrutiny. Who last scrutinized the way Her Majesty's Treasury operates? People don't! People who are on the inside will debate this . . . but there is probably more scrutiny of a secret agency than of a conventional government department."[42] The existence of the Investigatory Powers Commissioner's Office, the Intelligence and Security Committee, the Investigatory Powers Tribunal, and the Independent Reviewer of Terrorism Legislation does mean that there is a multilayered system of accountability, with each soliciting different amounts and types of information. Yet the secret nature of intelligence operations and the limited resources of oversight bodies means there are inbuilt constraints on their capacity to understand and analyze the full gamut of activity in this area.

Having outlined some of the formal reporting mechanisms that exist between the agencies and outside actors, whether that is the authorizing minister, the oversight bodies, or other organs of government, we now turn to the intra-agency processes of accountability. A system of rules and reporting procedures operates within each intelligence organization and is a crucial element of the formal understanding of accountability in this sphere. A former director general described the Security Service as "a machine which runs on a series of rules," implying that adherence to formal procedures was integral to its operations.[43] Their counterpart in SIS argued that "massively strong and rigorous procedures exist inside the Service, in terms of management and controlling staff" and "clear procedures in mounting any activity"[44]—a representation shared by former directors of GCHQ. As an example of how this operated in practice, a director general described the existence of a desk officer's "Manual of Investigations," which set out the requirements for approval from the head of your section or department, who "wouldn't sign it off if you hadn't made a proper case. They would send it back to you and you would have to do it again."[45] Operational practice was contrasted with fiction—"it isn't just like somebody on the telly pressing a button on a computer and up comes all this information. You have to have the correct authorizations"—and as a result, for the director general, "there was very strict control."[46] The key guiding questions in terms of seeking authorization and approving it were "Is it necessary to do this? Is it proper to do that?"[47] Thus, there is a practical and ethical component to the process.

Some kinds of activity also require the cooperation of other agencies, and so the need to account to outside parties for the reasons this action is necessary and proportionate provides a further practical element of accountability: "If you wanted to tap a phone, it's quite difficult to do it. You couldn't, as a desk officer, do it without lots of people knowing, and it being agreed, and the post office or British Telecom or whoever saying, it's possible, or technically difficult, or we can do it next Wednesday, or not today."[48] As the Security Service moved into the digital era, checks on database searches were introduced as well as a warning system, so that "if you were researching something outside of your area of work, it would put up a red flag and somebody would come along and ask you what you were up to."[49] In this way, digital oversight mechanisms allowed the agencies to identify suspect behavior and compel account-giving from their officials to justify their actions.

This mechanism continues to the present day. For instance, the now-defunct Interception of Communications Commissioner's Office (IOCCO) noted the safeguards on data analysis in GCHQ in its 2016 report: "my inspectors carry out random audit checks of the justifications for selection. In addition, GCHQ's Internal Compliance and IT security teams conduct audits to identify and further investigate any possible unauthorized use."[50] IOCCO was able to access these audits and received notice of any breaches identified. Awareness that activities could be subject to later auditing was described as a "strong safeguard" and "deterrent against malign use."[51] If suspect activity was found during these audits, the official would be called to account for their behavior and could be dismissed. However, the commissioner recommended these procedures be bolstered, either by wider auditing or more "preauthorization" of the selection of material, suggesting it was not seen as adequate as things stood.

In addition to organizational protocols, the legal framework surrounding investigatory powers is highly prescriptive about procedures in a way that is apparently unusual in normal legislation. A former security minister argues: "Not just what will be done but how it will be done is also in that law, and they regard that as a protection. If they follow the rules and the rules alone, it helps undermine the notion somehow that this is an organization that is potentially out of control."[52] This is a new development in the legal context for intelligence work, and means formal reporting mechanisms of accountability have the force of law in many cases. The level of autonomy for officials is thereby curtailed.

A further process reducing the freedom of action of intelligence officials is the extent to which they are integrated into a more complex system of intelligence-gathering in the digital era. While the Security Service has always had strong links with law enforcement and been subject to the constraints of operating in the domestic environment, SIS operatives historically enjoyed greater autonomy, and the organization fostered a more individualistic ethos. To some extent, this picture is a caricature, with a former chief of SIS seeing the service as "a very team-based organization, unlike any other government department."[53] However, Sir John Sawers, another former chief, depicts the SIS case officer in the field as formerly like "the sort of fighter pilot equivalent, the person around whom the whole intelligence operation revolved." In the digital era of big data, Sawers argues, "Now the case officer is just an implementer of plans that are developed back in head office, and the basis for those plans is analysis of big datasets." This is depicted as "one of the big changes that we have seen, in MI6 certainly, in the last ten years," and a "cultural transition."[54] Thus, it should be harder for individuals to "go rogue," as their actions are dictated by instructions from the center.

These kinds of accountability are generally concerned with ensuring that individuals do not utilize the resources of the state for personal reasons, to "look up your neighbor or your auntie or see if your girlfriend was on record."[55] While such abuses are important, they are relatively rare and face practical problems, as noted above. There is often the assumption that the essence of accountability is about rooting out bad individuals or poor decisionmaking at lower levels. As a former director of GCHQ argues, "You need a mechanism whereby information can get up to the levels at which people can do something about it if something needs to be done. The best kind of whistleblowing is internal, and it gets to senior management who did not know that this practice was going on and then intervene."[56] But what if the problem arises from policy decisions or managerial choices at a senior level? Where accountability via formal reporting faces challenge is if a group within the agency comes to operate in a dysfunctional manner, or where the system as a whole works against the public interest. The broader policy aspects are overseen by ministers, the Investigatory Powers Commissioner's Office, and the ISC; however, much of their activity relates to ensuring investigatory powers are used responsibly and within the framework of the law. There is less sense that some forms of activity may be narrowly legal but ethically wrong, and should be challenged on that basis.

Task-Oriented Accountability

When it comes to provoking accounts from within the national intelligence machinery and eliciting changes to behavior, one of the key motivating factors is often represented as the task at hand. The challenge of an evolving security environment means that officials are continually holding themselves to account and seeking to identify the most effective ways of achieving intelligence results.[57] This "task-oriented" accountability is a common framing of intelligence officials' explanations of what keeps them honest and motivated to perform to a high level. When asked what drives innovation, a director of GCHQ replied, "The task. . . . The task keeps changing. So the Cold War task led to a certain kind of fairly static organization, because that was the nature of the task. The post–Cold War world is very different, and has led to a very different kind of managerial outlook."[58] This framing is often defined as an aspect of accountability, linked to understandings of the term that emphasize being held to account, that is to say, being compelled to respond to criticism and reflect and learn from experience.[59]

Moreover, it is an ongoing and adaptive process. A former director general of the Security Service argues: "Accountability is there all the time. How do you define failure? Bombs go off, I guess is the most obvious example."[60] In this sense, there is an implied dialogue between the opponent and the agencies, and the success of the former necessarily leads to accountability of the latter for their failure. Reforms to formal accountability mechanisms in the past decade were largely driven by the failure to accurately map the threat environment. Thus, a former national security advisor asserts that the errors in intelligence reporting that occurred over Iraq—particularly, confusion over the processing—would not be possible now, as there is a clear chain of evidence on who did the analysis and how they arrived at their conclusions. Now, "You could go back to the JIC assessment, which is a written assessment, and say 'Where did this figure come from?'—and if there is an inquiry or a review by the ISC or someone else, they will be able to go back to the source and say, 'That is where that figure came from.' So that works pretty well now, but it only works so well now because there were failures in the past."[61]

Changes to intelligence practice in response to Iraq include both anticipatory and reflective elements. In terms of anticipating problems, the NSC has introduced more rigorous use of "red-teaming," involving "a set of experienced practitioners, coming up with their own policy options or trying to envisage how another country/organization might respond to the same situation."[62] The agencies had conducted internal "red" and "blue" team exercises to test operational assumptions prior to this,[63] but the NSC's involvement allows policy to be tested alongside operational choices. NSC country strategies now also include a section detailing country or regional triggers that might require a policy review—offering some scope for predicting emerging security threats.[64]

Befitting its focus on efficacy, task-oriented accountability also gives rise to extensive reflection on what worked or what went wrong in operations. At one level, this is a regularized aspect of operational activity. A current practitioner notes: "We have formal 'lessons learned' exercises all the time."[65] But it is also a reaction to the "perpetual crises," in which intelligence agencies find themselves. Following the London attacks in 2017, it is asserted that officials at every level of the organization would be asking themselves " 'Why did we miss it? Is there more we could have done? What more should we do?' All the way down to the most junior staff, you know, 'Give us ideas. What could we have done better?' So, that's what gets people up in the morning."[66]

If accountability is reactive, that automatically implies that there will be a time gap between any failure and the remedial response. As a former practitioner asserts, "The first thing to say about accountability is that it is something that is necessarily dynamic, it cannot be fixed. We cannot come up with a mechanism that will anticipate all contingencies, and there will be times when practice and reality are out of step with each other."[67] This is seen as happening during the immediate aftermath of the 9/11 attacks, with the desire to acquire intelligence taking precedence over human rights and legal constraints. This highlights one of the dangers of task-oriented accountability: that the desire not to risk failure could lead to overly extensive surveillance and intrusive activities, which ultimately may undermine the legitimacy of intelligence efforts. At present, officials believe the public do not see their operations as excessively impinging on their daily lives, but concede this is something they need to watch out for.

Vernacular Accountability

While the formal rules and institutionalized relationships outlined earlier are important to accountability, as is the context of continually evolving intelligence challenges, a vital component of its functioning lies in organizational culture. As an ethics counsellor of one of the intelligence agencies puts it, "Culture is the thing. It is the culture that keeps you honest. You must have rules, but without the right culture, rules would be an illusion."[68] Practitioners frequently emphasize that the agencies are nonhierarchical and have a "flat" structure, with few grades and significant interaction between senior and junior staff. A level of informality seems to have been in place since their early beginnings, with staff interacting on first-name terms and encouraged to express their opinions.[69] Whether intentional or not, the effect of this is to make account-giving and -receiving across the organization easier. A hierarchical structure could have exacerbated the effects of secrecy and produced a stratified bureaucracy with little interchange of ideas or reflective learning. By contrast, the sense conveyed by the interviewees is of a highly discursive space with staff frequently offering feedback and commentary on operational and policy matters.

For SIS, the experience of Iraq has given particular impetus to ensuring that this kind of culture flourishes. As Alex Younger, the current chief, states, "A vital lesson I take from the Chilcot report is the danger of groupthink. I will do anything I can to stimulate a contrary view; to create a culture where everyone has the confidence to challenge, whatever their seniority."[70] This kind of approach was adopted earlier by the Security Service and GCHQ. From the late 1990s onward, these two agencies invested considerable effort in canvassing the opinions of their staff and facilitating accounts to and from management about the running of their organizations, across a range of platforms. For instance, with the introduction of email, the director general of the Security Service instituted a policy whereby any member of staff could contact him directly, with protected anonymity, and he would commit to answering it, leading to three or four queries a week. An online discussion forum was introduced on the intranet, allowing staff to express their opinions about policy matters. The director general would wait to respond to allow the debate to develop: "If you go straight in with your boss's answer, that's not always helpful, so it may be better to leave it two or three days until some other people have joined in, and then that demonstrates that, actually, there are quite a lot of people thinking about this in the Service."[71] Ethical discussion was also fostered by the ethics counsellor, who would go around section meetings, raising points of concern and encouraging the airing of views. For the director general, the starting assumption was: "If we are going to get to the right point on these discussions, we need to do that through open dialogue."[72] Facilitating challenge was seen as vital to sustaining the "ethical buoyance" of the organization and managing the demands of intelligence and secrecy in a liberal democracy.

There is a preventive logic to this activity: "You want to get in there when people are thinking about what is and is not right and how things should or should not be done rather than waiting until something has gone wrong and blowing a whistle."[73] Thus, efforts to "shape the ethical climate of the Service" were, in part, stimulated by the desire to keep ethical debate in house. It is also interesting to consider what might constitute the "right point" to get to. A former director general asserts: "We would not change the policy on the basis of somebody's concerns unless, having discussed it and thought about it, considered it and looked at it, we decided the policy was wrong."[74] This does leave open the possibility of policy being changed; but more likely was the option that "If people had a real personal problem with an action, then we would accept that, ethically, from your perspective, you don't want to be involved in this, so we will do our best to ensure that you don't have to be."[75] This may work on a short-term basis, but long-term, if this was a core policy, it would be difficult for an individual to excuse themselves from operational involvement without damage to their career and working relationships—particularly since the Security Service is defined as a "one-team culture."[76]

Nevertheless, it is clear that a genuine attempt was made to foster ethical debate within the Security Service. In 2009, the ISC's annual report revealed that staff had gone to the ethics counsellor with a range of concerns since the post was created in 2006, including "whether the Service had adequate mechanisms to evaluate the mental and physical health risks to ICT agents; whether the Service should be involved in PREVENT work . . . whether it was ethical for the government to seek to alter the ideological views of its citizens . . . and whether there were sufficient controls for sharing information with countries that do not comply with international standards for the treatment of those in detention."[77] Many of these questions mirror those being asked in greater civil society debates at the time, and so reinforce the sense that the Service was open to external influence and did elicit serious ethical reflection from its staff.

A further cultural change was brought about as part of the agency's response to the 7/7 terrorist attacks in London in 2005, when it opted for "a completely different organizational construct based on regionalization rather than having a single headquarters down the river at Thames House."[78]

At the time, this was designed to meet the challenge of individuals being radicalized and turning to terrorism in the regions, and so was task oriented. However, it also had implications for vernacular accountability, since regionalization would be likely to increase the diversity of thought as well as the ethnic, religious, and class background of personnel. It is clear that geography is seen as important to organizational culture, with many interviewees noting that GCHQ's primary location in Cheltenham, away from London, meant that it was not subject to political or bureaucratic interference from Westminster or Whitehall compared to other government departments. It also opened a site in Manchester in 2019, in addition to existing offices in Bude, Cornwall, Scarborough, and Lincolnshire, as well as its subdivision, the National Cyber Security Centre, in Victoria, London. Thus, GCHQ is likely to see further diversity of the workforce and its ethical beliefs as these plans come to fruition.

GCHQ is perhaps the agency that has seen the greatest transformation in its culture and practices in the last two decades. Senior leaders in the organization recognized that technological change meant that they would require a very different management structure and set of practices to cope with the rapid growth in data and processing power of the digital era—as well as the changing demands of their consumers (primarily the Ministry of Defence). By the late 1990s, GCHQ was supposedly "not steerable from the top," due to a "rigid, silo-driven hierarchy," and producing "strategic intelligence—slow to process, and of value primarily to analysts in the end; analysts and MOD technical boffins in the defense scientific community, that sort of thing. It was geeks feeding geeks basically."[79] What the leadership aspired to was, as a former director put it, a "Silicon Valley–like organization," an informal workplace producing intelligence in a more innovative and nimble fashion that was of more immediate use to end users.[80] To achieve this change, their successor sought to inculcate a "listening culture," which entailed annual staff surveys and big "town hall meetings" with breakout sessions, allowing staff at the most junior level to "feed information upwards."[81] This was combined with a responsive management style, with leaders encouraged to seek out the opinions of colleagues across the hierarchy and increase the flows of information (accounts) cascading up and down the organization. The result was said to be that within a few years, GCHQ had transformed its working practices and moved from focusing overwhelmingly on strategic intelligence to "feeding real-time tactical information to commanders in the field," which is described as "a very, very different game."[82]

This system of open and free exchange of ideas has persisted in an era when the ethical demands of intelligence have become even more complex. An ethics counsellor argues: "If a new member comes in, they should challenge things and not just accept that is the way things are done . . . We have created an environment where people ask questions."[83] In practical terms, this is encouraged via informal meetings—"a 'stand up,' where you explain why you are doing this intelligence-gathering. Managers will encourage that."[84] In addition, "Some staff will be given an ethics role and operate as a 'force multiplier' " for the ethics counsellor.[85] Technology has presented GCHQ with a new set of ethical dilemmas when it comes to the development of artificial intelligence and machine learning. As a current practitioner puts it, "If you want to use this technology, then you will have to change how you do accountability. We will need to develop other ways of evaluating the consequences of what we do."[86] This may be done through modeling the likely outcomes or testing systems to check for biases and problems. It may also involve deciding not to use the technology "if humans cannot understand its implications," something "the whole of society is grappling with."[87]

Since this is viewed as a society-wide problem, GCHQ has engaged in dialogue with tech firms in the private sector, such as Microsoft, to see how they manage the ethical challenges of an era of neural networks, deep learning technology, and the possibility of "algorithmic drift," whereby systems evolve independently in ways that change or even subvert their creators' original intentions. The insight gleaned from Microsoft was that a diverse workforce was key. "If those who judge are a diverse group, then they are less likely to simply accept one view without question."[88] The assumption here is that diversity will also prevent unconscious gender, racial, or other biases from being implanted in AI systems. As noted in the introduction, GCHQ has been criticized in the past for having a culturally and ethnically narrow staff base and a severe gender imbalance, particularly at a senior level. The organization has sought assistance from activist groups like Stonewall to foster inclusivity, and is certainly making rhetorical effort to encourage recruitment from a more diverse pool of talent.[89]

In addition to engagement with the private sector and civil society, intelligence and security agencies have broadened the range of voices within their decisionmaking processes through extensive interagency cooperation and cross-Whitehall secondments. A number of respondents noted the transformative impact this has had on formerly stovepiped ways of working. As an ISC member put it, "Not only do they bring slightly different approaches to dealing with whatever the threat is you've been tasked with . . . they are checks on each other as well. You know, the way that an army lieutenant colonel from intelligence looks at something is going to be in a different way to a thirty-three-year-old lady working for GCHQ."[90] Thus, implied in this description is a sense that interaction across organizational boundaries creates intellectual and ethical challenges to ingrained assumptions.

A further source of diversity of opinion arises through the use of external consultancies. Firms such as Accenture or Deloitte have been brought in to provide managerial expertise and drive efficiency reforms. Their involvement in the everyday operations of the agencies is now a widespread practice and is seen as another consequence of avowal. According to a former national security advisor, "Since it is no secret that SIS exists, that GCHQ exists, they can work with those who can help them improve their HR and IT and so on, in the way that any other department can."[91] Indeed, a director general of the Security Service suggested: "We had as many pass-holders who were contractors as we had core members of the Service."[92] Thus, while the agencies operate behind a veil of secrecy, that does not preclude them from opening up their management practices to scrutiny from individuals from the private sector, with the proper clearance. These people can elicit accounts from officials at all levels of the organization and offer feedback and recommendations—thereby contributing to accountability in the sense of compelling individuals to provide an account and justification for their actions. However, it is done on an ad hoc basis and does not carry the formal weighting of Treasury or NAO evaluations discussed above.

This effort is important for vernacular accountability, since the determination of what types of account are provided and how they are received is a product of the cultural makeup of the organization in question. Racist and bigoted accounts were seen as acceptable in the intelligence agencies in the immediate postcolonial era due to the homogenous background of personnel. To ensure that there is robust challenge of intelligence policy in the coming age of AI, there will need to be a strong system of vernacular accountability in place, with contributions from individuals from a diverse range of backgrounds, questioning everyday practice and policy assumptions.

This may sound straightforward, but there are risks in implementing such reforms. Some practitioners noted that a more diverse workplace carries a greater risk of whistleblowing. Although this could also be seen as a positive, the implication was of whistleblowing that would be directed externally and undermine the reputation or working of the agency. If GCHQ really did become a Silicon Valley–like organization, rather than just simulate some of their practices, there would also be a risk that the ideological antipathy toward secrecy that permeates some of the tech culture on the West Coast of the United States might transfer to their operations. In such a scenario, there could be many more Edward Snowdens in the future.

From our discussion of how vernacular accountability operates in the national context, it seems apparent that secrecy is not a problem for organizational innovation. Spurred on by technological change, external political developments, or operational failures, the agencies have implemented cultural changes, which encourage challenge and questioning of operational practice and policy assumptions. These changes have brought forth a new system of vernacular accountability with a wider range of actors from the public and private sector sharing accounts, justifying decisions, and critiquing the use of intelligence in its many forms. As such, it is an important aspect of the overall accountability system governing the national intelligence machinery. But there is a question as to whether vernacular accountability lacks the anchoring of more formal reporting requirements. Imbalances of bureaucratic and political power will shape the extent and nature of dialogue, determining what gets discussed and what does not and whether any action flows from these debates.

To recap this chapter, the U.K. intelligence and security agencies have clearly undergone significant transformations in the formal accountability framework under which they operate. The key locus for authoritative account-giving and -receiving remains the minister, but new structures, such as the NSA and NSC, IPCO with its judicial commissioners, a reformed and enhanced ISC, as well as the Treasury and National Audit Office, all scrutinize their operations. The separate limitations of these oversight mechanisms have been noted, but collectively they represent a set of formal chains of accountability that work to shape and constrain intelligence practice. That said, this clearly does not capture the full complexity of account-giving and -receiving in the intelligence community. What keeps these organizations dynamic is, in part, the threat environment, with an implied dialogue of interaction between the agencies and their opponents. This self-generating momentum explains how the agencies are able to maintain their performance and drive change in the absence of comprehensive oversight. Yet the risk of such an approach to accountability dominating is that it may lead to an emphasis on efficacy over ethics. While this has been apparent on occasions, notably after 9/11, this impetus is kept in check by vernacular forms of accountability. The answer to the puzzle of what keeps secret organizations honest when external scrutiny is partial and they face severe operational demands arguably lies in internal culture and the myriad conversations about appropriateness and efficacy between colleagues.

FIVE

Liaison and International Intelligence Accountability

In the previous chapter we explored how members of the U.K. intelligence community understand accountability working in practice in a national context. However, to get a more complete sense of its functioning, it is important to analyze international as well as national mechanisms of accountability. In particular, it is necessary to consider how the United Kingdom shares intelligence with other states—through liaison relationships—and how this supports or undermines national accountability processes. Many security threats emanate from overseas, and so confronting them requires extensive intelligence-sharing, cooperation, and dialogue with external actors. These relationships also involve giving and receiving accounts, as well as notions of responsibility toward others and justification for actions. In this way, accountability operates beyond the confines of the domestic arrangements of nation-states like the United Kingdom. Following the same structure as the previous discussion, this chapter will analyze the formal reporting, task-oriented, and vernacular forms of accountability that exist at the international level. In doing so, it aims to tease out the similarities, differences, and overlaps between these processes and the ones identified in the national context. Analyzing liaison is more difficult than national intelligence practices, due to the sensitivity of these relationships. Many respondents would either not comment on how the United Kingdom interacts with other states or would not allow their views to be put on record. This account is therefore necessarily fragmentary and impressionistic, but aims to capture the essential elements of accountability in this context.

Formal Reporting

When it comes to the United Kingdom's intelligence relationships with other states, there are few formal reporting requirements. In a 2012 speech, the director of GCHQ asked the audience to reflect on the fact that "I talk of foreign colleagues as partners: they are neither our servants nor our masters."[1] The level of obligation to other states is very thin and self-interest is the dominant motivating factor in behavior. This means that even long-standing cooperative relationships, such as the United Kingdom–United States of America Agreement dating back to the Second World War, are viewed in highly transactional terms.

When it comes to intelligence-sharing, the only reporting obligation for participants is to provide sufficient information to justify their inclusion within the ring of secrecy of that particular network. As a former practitioner puts it, "The way intelligence works, if I were to go to the Americans and say, 'We would really like to know something about Ruritania, but we are not able to collect anything, can you help?,' the answer would be, 'We would love to help you, but we have got nothing.' Whereas if I were to go to the Americans and say, 'We are worried about Ruritania, so we have started a collection program and here is what we think . . . ,'' the Americans would say, 'Well, that is very interesting. We have got some reports that we can share with you.' That is how it works. It is always reciprocal. There are no free lunches."[2] This is not formal reporting in the sense of delegating authority and then seeking an account of how that authority was used, but it does link with formal mechanisms of account-giving and -receiving as set out in legal and institutional frameworks that govern intelligence-sharing—in this case, the United Kingdom–United States agreement and the "Five Eyes" network that overlays it. A former director of GCHQ frames the closeness of the United Kingdom's relationship with the United States as "entirely dependent on you delivering them, again, things that they want, and that is the most important form of accountability if you are running a secret agency."[3] In this sense, accountability is defined in terms of one's performance and contribution in a reciprocal relationship being judged as satisfactory.

In addition to reciprocity, there are two other governing norms that structure intelligence-sharing: namely, secrecy and the control principle. In relation to the first, William Hague noted, "If the countries we work with cannot trust us to protect their sources, then they will not share their information with us. We expect the same of them. We take it for granted in diplomacy that we must uphold our agreements and respect the confidences of our partners."[4] This norm suffered a legal challenge when the U.K. government was ordered by the Court of Appeal in 2010 to release a seven-paragraph summary of classified CIA information relating to the interrogation of Binyam Mohammed.[5] The government had argued against this decision, but there were still severe political consequences for the United Kingdom–United States relationship. The original ruling in 2009 decided against releasing the information after the United States threatened to withdraw intelligence cooperation and a letter was sent from the U.S. intelligence community, following the appeal, making it clear that negative actions would follow should this be repeated. An ISC member recalls speaking to the CIA soon afterward and finding "they were really annoyed that their intelligence had been used in open court in that case and they were just quite rude. It was not that the intelligence service volunteered it; the courts demanded it . . . I remember one of them saying, 'If someone is about to blow up central London, we will cooperate with you. Anything else, forget it.' "[6] It is possible to see this reaction as a form of accountability, with the United Kingdom having to provide an account in defense of its breach of confidence and the United States implying that punishment will follow if negative behavior occurs in the future.

This case was not only important for secrecy reasons, but also because it linked to the longstanding "control principle" governing the use of intelligence. As a former national security advisor explains, the control principle means, "the originator of the intelligence is responsible for the dissemination of that intelligence."[7] In practice, that means that other states are not supposed to share, disclose, or act upon intelligence without clearing it first with the originator. To do so, states have to report back to the originator on their handling of intelligence, and so a formalized social norm of account-giving and -receiving is instituted during these transactions. As noted above, this is not a legal requirement but a social convention, and is violated at times, either by accident or by design. Indeed, the United States contravened the principle in relation to intelligence supplied to them by the United Kingdom in the Mubanga case in 2002.[8] When this is pointed out, the common response is that such double standards underline the asymmetry between the United Kingdom and the United States in their intelligence partnership.

In sum, reciprocity, secrecy, and the control principle provide a structure to account-giving processes between states. Violation of these norms can lead to agencies being held to account and facing sanction from those who perceive themselves to have been wronged. Discussion of asymmetries leads us to consider the hierarchies of account-giving between states. In the United Kingdom's conceptualization of its intelligence relationships, the United Kingdom–United States relationship is of paramount importance, followed by the rest of the "Five Eyes" network (Canada, Australia, and New Zealand). France and Germany are often cited next, though some posit the Netherlands as superior to Germany. These states are also important to European networks such as the CTG group of thirty states cooperating over counterterrorism. Beyond that, there are a series of bilateral cooperative relationships with developing countries, which in the past have been seen as secondary but can achieve momentary importance, depending on the issue at hand.[9]

In this regard, 9/11 is viewed as a seminal moment. A former practitioner explains: "Before 9/11, there was a clear hierarchy . . . at that point, engagement with services in the developing world was more about making sure that you had the right to undertake independent operations with the concurrence of the state in question and also about exercising political influence."[10] Since heads of intelligence and security services in the developing world were often figures of significant power, the U.K. agencies engaged with them in order to pursue diplomatic interests. After 9/11, this rather distant approach was transformed: "All of a sudden, you saw the beginnings of a high-tempo operational collaboration of a whole bunch of services with whom we had had very little up until that particular juncture, and needed to work with them in a very different way. And the fact that they operated by different rules and had different ethical standards was often a problem, in Pakistan in particular."[11] Thus, the hierarchy was overturned and the United Kingdom found itself having to prioritize relationships with states that demanded reciprocity, not just over intelligence but the wider spectrum of interactions.

Indeed, intelligence cooperation was, at times, framed as conditional on the United Kingdom's willingness to bend its own rules and turn a blind eye to suspected corruption by elites in partner countries. In the most public case, in 2006, Saudi Arabia threatened to withdraw intelligence cooperation with the United Kingdom unless the British government dropped a Serious Fraud Office investigation into the Al-Yamamah arms deal between the two countries. The prime minister, Tony Blair, agreed to do so, and the attorney general defended the decision in Parliament on national security grounds, asserting that "the wider public interest . . . outweighed the need to maintain the rule of law."[12] In this way, an intelligence partner was holding Britain to account (in terms of maintaining the secrecy of their defense arrangements) while at the same time subverting the United Kingdom's domestic legal accountability mechanisms.

Difficulties arose over liaison relationships with other states, particularly when intelligence interests overlapped with those of the United States. As a former high commissioner recalls, "there was a time when the question of accountability was most personal to us all, because we operated in a very different legal environment from the United States . . . it was made aware to me that I could be made personally liable if intelligence that we passed to the Pakistanis, for instance, was used in a way that was illegal or violated our accountability procedures."[13] There are tensions evident here, though, between different forms of obligation. SIS was keen to obtain information to protect the safety of U.K. citizens and, as noted, partner agencies expect reciprocity. In addition, the United Kingdom has legal obligations under the UN Security Council Resolutions 1373 (2001) and 1624 (2005), to cooperate with other states on counterterrorism. Yet they also have legal responsibilities as a signatory to the UN Convention against Torture and other Cruel, Inhuman or Degrading Treatment or Punishment 1984, and its Optional Protocol, not to facilitate or encourage others to commit such acts. In addition, they are subject to the European Convention on Human Rights, incorporated into domestic law via the Human Rights Act 1998.

In other words, there is a legal framework of accountability in place and, as the high commissioner notes, this applies to individuals as well as states. At least three police investigations were launched to look into the actions of individual officials in the war on terror period: Operation Hinden, into a Security Service officer who interrogated Binyam Mohammed, an al-Qaeda suspect, in Pakistan; Operation Iden, into an SIS officer who interrogated suspects at Bagram prison in Afghanistan; and Operation Lydd, into the Libya rendition case, where the SIS Officer involved, Mark Allen, faced a potential prosecution for his remarks about the transfer of detainees until the case was eventually dropped.[14] A former national security advisor suggests of Allen that "as a senior MI6 officer, he might never have expected to be sort of vulnerable from a legal point of view."[15] In light of this tightening of the legal controls, "everyone takes the whole legal framework very seriously."[16] Thus, liaison relationships became highly problematic after 2001, as officials sought to balance the expectations and requirements of allies with the denser legal framework that had emerged after the Cold War.

That said, legal accountability at the international level remains fragmentary and heavily reliant on the cooperation of states. During the war on terror period, the United Kingdom faced considerable criticism from human rights groups, as well as being included in investigations by the United Nations,[17] the Council of Europe,[18] and the European Union about activities associated with torture, detention, and rendition. As noted in chapter 2, it did offer accounts in response, frequently declaring that it did not condone or encourage torture. On the basis of evidence from the United States, it had denied that its air bases had been used to facilitate renditions in this era, subsequently correcting this account in 2008, when the United States admitted that two flights had passed through the British base in Diego Garcia. The Council of Europe's lead investigator, Dick Marty, stated in his report in 2007: "The U.K. government has readily accepted assurances from U.S. authorities to the contrary, without ever independently or transparently inquiring into the allegations itself, or accounting to the public in a sufficiently thorough manner."[19] Thus, it faced opprobrium from external sources about how far it had become complicit in torture and rendition and failed to demonstrate accountability for its actions. This kind of criticism was eventually part of the justification for launching the Gibson inquiry. Nevertheless, the international impact on state practice can often be limited. As an illustration of the context in which international bodies struggle to elicit accounts from states on their behavior, the UN special rapporteur on torture, Manfred Nowak, noted in 2005 that "Of 1,000 urgent action claims sent to Governments, more than 60 percent of them had not responded."[20]

More effective are regional efforts in Europe to hold governments to account, since European states operate within a tighter legal framework, including having courts that are able to arrive at binding judgments on state parties. The European Court of Human Rights fined Romania, Lithuania, Poland, and Italy for their actions in supporting aspects of the rendition and torture regime implemented by the United States after 9/11.[21] Compliance with regional legal standards is based on practical as well as reputational bases. A current practitioner asserts that "The EU would not want to work with us if we did not handle data correctly."[22] Furthermore, EU partners have sought assurances from the United Kingdom that their intelligence was not used in torture, with the implication that sharing would stop if this was suspected.[23] Thus, the desire to comply with legal norms sets off trains of account-giving and -receiving as part of the intelligence-sharing process.

The United Kingdom, in turn, has sought assurances from its partners and engaged in close dialogue over their practices to ensure legal compliance; for instance, when it comes to intelligence cooperation with the United States linked to their program of targeted killing of terrorists.[24] In short, there are elements of reporting and institutionalized account-giving and -receiving being undertaken in liaison relationships, with the potential for partners to be held to account were they to breach their obligations.

A final, important, point to make about formal lines of intelligence accountability is that it would be wrong to portray the United Kingdom as always the most regulated and rule-guided actor in any liaison relationship. From 1974, the United States congress asserted control over covert action by U.S. agencies and demanded that no funds be spent until the president had notified key committees about the intended activity and its justification in each case.[25] Since then, notes Rory Cormac, SIS has provided a useful route for the CIA to avoid congressional oversight, since the latter's links with U.K. intelligence could be badged as liaison rather than covert action.[26]

Cormac describes how during the 1980s, the CIA would funnel money to SIS to "channel silencers to Afghanistan, effectively funding assassination," and quotes a CIA officer, Gust Avrakotos, arguing SIS "had a willingness to do jobs I couldn't touch. They basically took care of the How to Kill People Department."[27] More recently, SIS is said to have helped the CIA get around reporting covert action to congress in 2012 by facilitating the transfer of weapons from Libya into Syria.[28] Thus, liaison can function as a means to avoid formal accountability mechanisms, and this is a two-way street between the United Kingdom and its liaison partners.

Task-Oriented Accountability

Intelligence liaison relationships are highly purposive, and therefore it is unsurprising that there is a lot of task-oriented account-giving and -receiving taking place. In the first instance, officials wish to appear competent in the eyes of their liaison partners, and so this can motivate them to hold themselves to a high standard. One former SIS officer argues: "Being in a liaison relationship should ensure that you really are performing at your best because you do not want those guys to see you slip up."[29] The density of this practice seems to reflect the hierarchy of intelligence-sharing noted earlier, with the "Five Eyes" network dominating, then European agencies, and more peripheral ones impinging on an ad hoc basis. "Five Eyes" substructures were seen as useful for "getting the best technical answers to common problems."[30] The Canadians, Australians, and New Zealanders, as smaller outfits, focused on a rather smaller set of operational targets but were often, for that reason, able to devise specialized solutions. A director of GCHQ recalls: "Whenever I went and met . . . with my Canadian and Australian opposite number, I was very careful to try and discover how they were approaching their tasks—because we were all essentially facing the same challenges—to see whether any of their innovations might be scalable."[31] Thus, interchange would occur and their advice would be canvassed, but the key liaison relationship for task-oriented accountability was and is the United States.[32]

As noted above, the United Kingdom places significant importance on demonstrating its usefulness to this relationship. All three agencies indicated the significance of the United States to their operations, but this was particularly the case for GCHQ, which worked very closely with their counterparts in the U.S. National Security Agency. The NSA is a much larger organization than GCHQ (perhaps four or five times as big), very well-resourced and "extremely generous in passing over knowhow about how you get technology to work."[33] They are also deeply embedded in the operational aspects of GCHQ's work in terms of physical presence. As a director of GCHQ describes it, "A great deal of the closeness of liaison arrangements depended enormously on flows of personnel as well as on you keeping your customers happy. We had a lot of people embedded in the NSA. NSA had a lot of people embedded in us. Measured in tens rather than hundreds. Quite a lot of tens, and not just all in one place but scattered around in different places, too."[34] Indeed, this cross-fertilization of ideas and exchange of people between GCHQ and NSA is seen as so important that their predecessor asked whether reform of their organization would have been possible in the NSA's absence—an "interesting question" that they go on to implicitly answer by emphasizing this as the third of three factors driving change, behind geographical location and internal culture.[35]

Beyond these institutionalized and longstanding relationships, the U.K. intelligence agencies share accounts with other services on an ad hoc basis. In the immediate post–Cold War era, U.K. officials poured into ex-Soviet states and had extensive conversations about tradecraft, learning a number of useful surveillance techniques. In return, they gave advice and training on developing appropriate intelligence and security services for a liberal democratic setting. This conveys the possibility of these agencies having a positive effect on democratic societies, when the right balance is struck between surveillance and privacy, government power and citizens' rights. Contrary to the dominant view of counterterrorism negatively affecting global human rights norms,[36] it is even argued that in some cases, task-oriented accountability in intelligence-sharing arrangements helps to uphold the norm against torture. One interviewee suggested that liaison with Pakistan could often involve exhortations to respect humanitarian norms, with SIS officials arguing: "Look, if you do it your way, this is going to achieve no result for us, because we are after a court case, and if you do it your way, no judge is going to entertain it."[37] Margaret Beckett suggests that the Attorney General Peter Goldsmith visited Pakistan and "talked to their police and their judiciary and so on," arguing, "'Look, you cannot do this,' or 'this is no use to us, because we have to be able to show what the British courts will consider valid evidence obtained in a valid way.' "[38] This argument was conveyed in transactional terms, as a "two-way street," since Pakistan also wished to extradite individuals, and in response to their question "why can't you just send us these people?," British policymakers would state: "we can't send you these people because you haven't supplied us with something that our courts will consider evidence."[39] Thus, formal legal norms were bolstered by the argument that it was necessary to abide by them in order to pursue operational goals.

The United Kingdom has also had fruitful dialogues with the Israeli security services, including early notice of the usefulness of data analytics, which the U.K. Security Service was eventually able to capitalize on and develop in its own right. In the context of the Counterterrorism Group, the United Kingdom works closely with European agencies on developing their counterterrorism tactics, "working together jointly on investigations and collection operations to deliver results and disruptions," as well as jointly developing methodologies to spot "lone actor" terrorists.[40] Respondents were generally reluctant to go on the record about either the scope of this exchange, the techniques shared, or the prioritization of particular countries or threats. Israel is clearly seen as a special case, in terms of its technical performance and level of innovation, and is ranked higher than U.K. agencies in that regard by some interviewees. European states offer niche capabilities in some areas, but are not perceived as operating at the same level of expertise—with the possible exception of the French intelligence services, which are marked out as acting under a uniquely permissive domestic environment, free from the oversight and constraints of the United Kingdom.

Overall, the sense from the interviewees is that task-oriented accountability is most pertinent to the United Kingdom's relationship with the United States. Officials are particularly concerned about how their performance is perceived by this intelligence partner, and the densest pattern of interactions, including information-sharing and personnel secondment, occurs with their American counterparts. Given how valued this relationship is across the national intelligence community, it is perhaps not surprising that the United Kingdom was slow to distance itself from the United States' counterterrorism efforts after 9/11, despite their use of detention and interrogation techniques that were contrary to U.K. and international law.

Vernacular Accountability

Beyond specific tasks, accountability is also shaped by the milieu of intelligence cooperation, with officials from liaison services working closely together, via secondments and exchanges. Inhabiting each other's cultures and practices imbues officials, over time, with a shared sense of what is appropriate or effective. Again, contrary to the notion that secrecy leads to closed organizational cultures, a former national security advisor states that "the 'Five Eyes' sit on the JIC for certain issues, and our representatives in Washington are part of the American intelligence assessment process."[41] In a 2018 speech, Andrew Parker, director general of the Security Service, set out in detail the cooperative arrangements between his officials and their European counterparts, asserting that "the vast majority of my intelligence officers will spend huge chunks of their careers working collaboratively with European colleagues," with networks like the CT group entailing "thousands of exchanges on advanced secure networks every week."[42] In addition, the United Kingdom conducts joint exercises with partner agencies in France, the Netherlands, and Germany, and canvasses their advice on issues where their knowledge is seen as more advanced—as in discussions with the French services in the mid-1990s, as the threat from Islamist extremism began to emerge in Europe.[43]

A former security minister describes the benefit of this sort of activity as "mind-clearing." "You know they talk to each other about the meaning of all of this, too, about what the political significance of it is . . . having another government and another political context, one which you trust and can bat ideas, bat them about, and how you add up the bits of the jigsaw that you have got . . . it is quite helpful."[44] At times, the Security Service has drafted in external experts from the "Five Eyes" community to conduct peer reviews of their operations. A former director general noted the political challenges of selecting a candidate who could offer a suitably rigorous assessment of operational performance while being trustworthy and sensitive to the environmental constraints under which officials were operating. In the case they recalled, it was a "recently retired deputy of the Australian service," who came in for two or three months, reviewed the operational capabilities of the Service, and noted positive aspects as well as areas where learning was required.[45] This sort of peer review is not uniformly practiced.

A former chief of SIS rejected on national security grounds the idea of their organization allowing external scrutiny by individuals from another country, even one from a "Five Eyes" state. On the evidence of the interviews conducted for this project, and the rare public statements of heads of the intelligence and security agencies, there seems to be far more cooperative working and account-giving and -receiving between GCHQ and the Security Services and their international counterparts than is the case for SIS.

Overall, vernacular accountability among intelligence and security services at the international level is seen as positive, as long as it involves information exchange with states that enjoy the confidence of officials and are perceived to share the values of U.K. intelligence practitioners. But the range of partners that fulfill these criteria is limited. There is also a reluctance to risk losing operational advantage by spreading knowledge of tradecraft too widely. Furthermore, liaison relationships with foreign intelligence and security services are seen as carrying the risk of subverting domestic legal or ethical norms—or misdirecting intelligence efforts away from U.K. national interests. A former security minister states that liaison "can lead you up the garden path"—something they felt had occurred over Iraq, where the closeness of interchange between the United States and the United Kingdom had fed the groupthink that led to war.

Unlike vernacular accountability in the national context, there is little sense of civil society influencing intelligence practice on a global level. International activist groups and governance bodies are not even mentioned by respondents; nor are multinational firms, at least in relation to global interactions. As noted in chapter 3, international intelligence activities are not conveyed as subject to the same levels of legal or political scrutiny as domestically focused tasks. Therefore, it appears that there are fewer mechanisms for account-giving and -receiving globally, compared to those that exist at the national level. A necessary caveat to any conclusions about the extent of vernacular accountability between actors internationally is the fact that respondents may not wish to speak openly about them with the interviewer in case this was seen as breaching the confidence of the foreign liaison partners. A number of comments on these relationships were offered "off the record." Even so, the desire to maintain secrecy and the competitive nature of global intelligence work do seem to inhibit the free exchange of information on techniques, norms, and ways of working between U.K. agencies and their counterparts abroad. Rather, when intelligence is shared, it is usually conveyed in a form that masks the methods and motives that led to its acquisition. As Margaret Beckett puts it, "The one thing they never tell you is how they got the information—and you don't either . . . They just tell you, 'Here is this bit of information,' with whatever detail they want you to look at. They don't tell you whether they got it from a telephone. They don't tell you whether they got it from human intelligence; that somebody you know told them this. They don't tell you whether somebody was ill-treated to get it. Why would they? They just don't."[46] Thus, while vernacular accountability does take place and can involve some detailed information-sharing with close intelligence partners, the normal pattern of intelligence liaison is of limited exchange of knowledge, to preserve secrecy.

Conclusion

This book addresses one of the most prominent dilemmas of modern governance: how can intelligence and security agencies be held accountable when much of what they do is secret and hence inscrutable? The consequences of intelligence failings, as outlined in chapter 2, can be severe, with the United Kingdom embarking on a war in Iraq in 2003 on a false intelligence prospectus, being complicit in torture and ill treatment of terrorist suspects as part of the war on terror, underestimating the threat from hostile states such as Russia, and failing to prevent terrorist attacks at home and abroad. For that reason, it is important to consider how oversight bodies and the public can ensure that intelligence organizations are working effectively in the public interest, and acting in accordance with British society's values. It is also a vital question, because the agencies' ways of working are undergoing transformational change due to technological developments. How the power of the digital world and artificial intelligence is understood, utilized, and regulated goes to the heart of the functioning of the United Kingdom as a liberal democratic state. To understand how these changes will be managed, the public needs a much firmer appreciation of the way intelligence accountability operates and how it could be improved.

I began the discussion by considering how accountability is understood in the academic literature, and the challenges secrecy presents—both in terms of rendering accounts and holding actors to account for their actions. I then investigated intelligence accountability in the United Kingdom, analyzing how scrutiny bodies have highlighted problems and dilemmas in this area in terms of policy, operational performance, efficiency, and ethics. I complemented this public appraisal of the work of the U.K. intelligence and security agencies with an investigation into practitioners' private understanding of the concept of accountability and its application. Using original interview data, I analyzed the beliefs and assumptions about how accountability works in the everyday world of intelligence and security practice.

A number of insights emerged from this discussion, with implications for both the broad study of intelligence accountability and the U.K. case in particular. First, secrecy does not necessarily translate into closed bureaucratic systems. It is clear from the interviewees' responses that there is considerable cross-fertilization of ideas and personnel across agencies and across national boundaries. That may provide one explanation for why the abuse of intelligence power is not more common, at least in liberal democratic states: there are too many interested parties for malpractice to stay secret for long.

Second, accountability carries significant benefits for organizations. Giving and receiving accounts involves sharing knowledge and expertise, which improves performance. It can also act as a safety valve for internal dissent. As revealed in chapter 4, allowing personnel to express unease or dissatisfaction with aspects of intelligence work is seen as a positive form of challenge to potentially unethical policy directions and reduces the chance of whistleblowing to outside agencies (thereby preserving the integrity of the secret intelligence system as a whole).

Third, while much of the academic focus on intelligence accountability looks at formal mechanisms of external oversight, this is only one aspect of how accountability operates in this area. Indeed, for practitioners, the most salient forms of account-giving and -receiving are often intrinsic, involving dialogue with peers, or partner agencies abroad, about everyday practices.

Therefore, this study broadened the focus of analysis from solely formal institutional oversight to identify three separate ways of articulating accountability. In the first place, those formal mechanisms were acknowledged. Accountability was related to formal chains of reporting, often concerning delegated authority. For some respondents, these remain the essence of accountability, and other forms of account-giving should be excluded or redefined as something else; however, this understanding is by no means universal. In many of the interviews, the world of intelligence was conveyed as uniquely dynamic, due to the imperative to counter ever-evolving security threats. Thus, I posited a second, "task-oriented" accountability, whereby account-giving and -receiving takes place instrumentally (often in response to crises), to improve performance or identify solutions to technical problems. Intelligence work is depicted as adaptive and reactive, and much of the focus of appraising the actions of officials is related to how far they achieve their objectives.

These two forms of accountability generally emerge from external stimuli, but my analysis of the interview data also revealed a third system, which was more internal and informal in its genesis and development: vernacular accountability. Officials engage in everyday deliberations on the nature of intelligence practice, on the appropriateness of policy and operational decisions, on which threats should be prioritized and which downgraded, and on the ethical boundaries for action. Looking only at external scrutiny or reactions to external events risks missing out on how internal beliefs, norms, and routines shape practice. This concept links with Aldrich and Richterova's idea of "ambient accountability," in that the environmental context is important, but focuses in particular on the articulations and discursive interactions of participants.[1]

Inevitably, these frames overlap, but each implies a distinct set of accountability questions for officials. Accountability via formal reporting begs the questions: have I followed instructions and done what is expected of me? Were my actions in accordance with my lawful authority? For task-oriented accountability, the questions would be: have I performed a task well? How could I achieve my objectives better next time? Meanwhile, vernacular accountability asks: what would be appropriate or ethical behavior in this context? How does what we do fit with the culture and norms of our organization, or wider society? How do our actions compare with those of others? The first emphasizes authority, the second efficacy, and the third ethics. These three categories are more useful than the usual tripartite structure of efficiency, effectiveness, and ethics found in the literature, as efficiency is actually a subcategory of the wider principal-agent relationships associated with authority as well as discussions on effectiveness. The importance of delegated authority and its implications for liberal democracy are such that formal reporting requirements, I would argue, merit their own category of analysis.

In short, these new categories allow a fuller appreciation of the range of account-giving and -receiving in the intelligence realm and contribute to our understanding of what motivates intelligence professionals to act ethically, and ensure they are performing effectively, despite the limited nature of external oversight.

Lessons for Future U.K. Intelligence Accountability

Having explored the theoretical repercussions of this research, I now turn to the practical implications for the U.K. intelligence machinery. The audit of the performance of the intelligence and security agencies in chapter 2 reveals three areas for improvement. First, there is a need to develop and enhance the agencies' anticipatory capability. Most of the major developments in world politics over the last two decades—from 9/11 to the Arab Spring, from the Russian intervention in Ukraine to the emergence of the Islamic State—apparently came as a surprise to the intelligence services; indeed, intelligence activity in the Maghreb was being downgraded just as the Arab Spring broke out.[2] As a former director of GCHQ characterizes it: "The whole sort of central machinery was essentially reactive, and there was nobody looking for, there was no voice speaking for, tomorrow's threat."[3] According to a former national security advisor, "The government is pretty good, by and large, at dealing with current threats, but it is not good at foreseeing the next one and the one after that," and this is viewed as "an area of weakness and always has been."[4] The NSC have incorporated "specific country/regional triggers likely to require a policy review" into their country strategies,[5] but a more systematic and substantial process is required. One of the purposes of intelligence services is to provide informational advantage about upcoming threats and challenges, and it is clear that the U.K. agencies have not been effective in this regard during the period under scrutiny. The Ministry of Defence conducts analysis of emerging trends likely to affect warfare in the future.[6] The national intelligence machinery clearly needs to replicate and develop this kind of horizon-scanning to anticipate emerging security challenges or opportunities. The JIC is supposed to combine the insights of the agencies and identify security threats as they develop, but it is apparent that this body mostly functions in a reactive manner.

Second, the continual reporting of errors and mistakes that have been highlighted by numerous ISC investigations suggest that poor record-keeping is an ongoing problem. The agencies clearly need to remedy this aspect of their performance, as having an accurate record system whose search function is effective would seem an essential aspect of intelligence work. It is also vital to holding the intelligence and security services to account. Without it, accounts offered are either incomplete or absent. As a nontechnical external observer, I am not in a position to suggest detailed solutions, but the recurrence of this issue over such an extended time indicates that it has not received sufficient bureaucratic attention. Nor is this simply attributable to agencies' unwillingness to share their knowledge with oversight bodies. As was apparent in chapter 2, record searches failed, even when it would have been in the agencies' interests to disclose information.

Third, the war on terror period gave rise to a set of ethical challenges that are still affecting intelligence practice today. This is usually framed in terms of the United Kingdom having to develop deeper collaborative working relationships with countries that do not share Britain's values—exposing them to charges of complicity in torture and the mistreatment of detainees.[7] This framing is problematic, partly because U.K. officials clearly facilitated and encouraged such practices in their drive to acquire intelligence—particularly in the years immediately after 9/11. In addition, Britain's closest intelligence partner, the United States, was a key actor in the development of an international system that tortured and mistreated detainees.[8] To understand and respond to the ethical dilemmas of countering international terrorism, all three of the main intelligence and security services instituted a culture of questioning among their staff. This was implemented through formal mechanisms like the staff and ethics counsellor, but also through ad hoc and informal means like staff forums, surveys, and "stand ups" (see chapter 4). Such a system should hopefully avoid the silences observed among personnel when mistreatment was being discussed in early 2002 (see chapter 2).

The government has revised its "Consolidated Guidance to Intelligence Officers and Service Personnel on the Detention and Interviewing of Detainees Overseas, and on the Passing and Receipt of Intelligence Relating to Detainees" a number of times.[9] The extent to which the contemporary intelligence environment gives rise to dilemmas over cooperation is apparent from the intelligence and security commissioner's report in 2016, which noted that the agencies had consulted the guidance on 921 occasions—failing to apply it properly in 35 cases, 8 of which "should have prohibited further action—presumably as a result of what were serious risks of torture or other ill-treatment."[10] One issue that emerges from the interviews with former and current practitioners is the extent to which ethical discussion occurs within organizational silos—rather than across the national intelligence machinery. This disconnect means that account-giving that might be useful for other agencies is not shared, and so the overall system lacks the benefit of a whole of government approach to managing the ethical challenges of intelligence. An obvious means of correcting this might be for online forums to be open to staff from all three intelligence and security services to comment on and read.

When one considers the impact of the three different forms of accountability, it becomes clear that formal reporting structures of accountability do have a marginal but important effect. As a former chief of SIS puts it, "They ginger your attitude, your focus on things."[11] On the one hand, this means that the intelligence and security services feel compelled to respond when their attention is drawn to particular instances of poor or unethical performance—as over the treatment of detainees or the use of intelligence to justify war in Iraq in 2003. The downside of such responsiveness is it tends to reflect the prejudices and interests of scrutiny bodies. Serious gaps in the availability and exploitation of intelligence in Afghanistan in 2006, the Arab Spring in 2011, or Russian intervention in Ukraine in 2014 are only lightly examined by the oversight bodies, and so have not elicited reflection from the national intelligence machinery.

With regard to legal controls over the use of surveillance powers, there is now a more robust regime in place than the one that existed before. IPCO has enhanced powers and seems to be conducting inspections as well as approving warrants in a rigorous fashion. That said, its remit across all the public bodies that exercise surveillance powers (with the exception of local authorities in Northern Ireland) means its attention is arguably spread thin. Moreover, there is clearly a gap in the scrutiny of overseas actions, which either fall under class authorizations or are excluded from judicial oversight altogether. It is questionable how far this is sustainable in the future, since intelligence actions overseas expose the government and wider society to reputational and practical risks. There does not seem a firm logic as to why scrutiny should be lighter internationally. Even if the legal framework is not as dense, the organizations would likely benefit from feedback and reviews of operational practice by properly vetted external parties.

One area that arguably needs further reform is the Investigatory Powers Tribunal. The paucity of references to this body among interviewees suggests it has little or no impact on intelligence practice and is not a prominent feature of their understanding of accountability in the United Kingdom. Given how important it should be, as a vital conduit for public complaints against the intelligence and security services, this needs to be corrected. Building on the discussion in chapter 2, there are some radical solutions that could be tried in order to bolster the tribunal's salience within the national intelligence machinery. One possibility could be a legally prescribed duty for officials to report malfeasance to the tribunal. The tribunal could, in turn, notify injured parties, subject to the constraints of secrecy and national security concerns. This would introduce a more robust system for identifying misconduct than the current ad hoc mechanism by which individuals have to suspect wrongdoing against themselves in the first place, before an investigation is launched. Going even further, the government could introduce positive financial incentives for whistleblowers, although this may have a negative impact on staff morale. Social psychologists have noted that financial incentives can have counterintuitive results.[12] In this case, they may lessen the sense of public duty, which should motivate whistleblowing, in favor of self-interest. One downside of this might be that staff do not report wrongdoing through the proper channels in the first instance, so as to increase their chances of getting a payout from the external body.

The difficulties the IPT has encountered in allowing the public to challenge the actions of the intelligence and security services underlines how elite-focused are the current formal mechanisms of accountability. As noted in chapter 1, legitimacy is a vital part of intelligence work.[13] The current chief of SIS argues: “Everything we do at MI6, we do in the public’s name. It follows that a vital underpinning of our work is public confidence.”[14] Having ordinary people take part in ethical discussion with officials could be a useful tool in demonstrating that the national intelligence machinery is sensitive and responsive to public opinion. Therefore it stands to reason that public involvement in policy should be facilitated wherever possible, so that the agencies can ensure the work they do reflects the values and interests of the society they represent.

To enable this, the national intelligence machinery could consider following the lead of the health service in the United Kingdom, which makes use of research ethics committees. These bodies “review research proposals to assess formally if the research is ethical. This means the research must conform to recognized ethical standards, which includes respecting the dignity, rights, safety, and well-being of the people who take part.”[15] About a third of each committee is made up of lay people working on a voluntary basis, and the rest are experts with specific knowledge that will allow them to explain and evaluate research proposals. There are over eighty such committees in operation at present across the United Kingdom. They aim to give a decision within sixty days, with most committees offering a response within forty. The important thing about their existence is they allow the general public to have an input into what kinds of medical research are allowed, while at the same time demonstrating that lay people can have a constructive role in appraising even highly technical scientific work.

Although these committees have had issues over delays in the past,[16] they do seem to function well and could be replicated in other fields. An intelligence ethics committee system would allow the intelligence and security services to check proposals to expand or modify their intelligence collection techniques or policies. Mirroring research ethics committees, it might consist of security-cleared lay volunteers, as well as former practitioners, academics, and law enforcement personnel with technical or professional knowledge that qualifies them to assist in the committee’s judgments. The kinds of questions it may address include the use of artificial intelligence in targeted surveillance and offender profiling, bulk data capture, agent running, and the thresholds for intelligence-sharing with other countries. Such a system would allow the intelligence and security services to verify that their practices are in accordance with the values of wider society, provide useful feedback on the ethical dilemmas of operations, and offer a check on bureaucratic momentum. That way, if powers are extended or technology used in a more expansive manner, it will at least have happened as a result of conscious choices.

This facility would also enhance the existing system, since the ISC and IPT are designed to offer retrospective commentary on the performance of the intelligence and security services rather than anticipatory judgments. At present, the only outside body in place to offer advice or feedback on intelligence techniques or operational plans in this way is the staff counsellor and so the discussion is, at present, very inwardly focused. It is also, arguably, too much for one individual to be expected to represent the opinions of wider society. Judicial commissioners approve warrants in advance, but not policy choices—those are left to the minister, who, as argued earlier, has a limited capacity to engage on such matters in depth.

It is perhaps surprising that a number of practitioners have expressed approval for the idea of the general public having more direct input into intelligence accountability. In the interviews, a former chief of SIS argued, "There should be a citizen's body which didn't authorize warrants but scrutinized them on a selective basis."[17] Meanwhile, a former director of GCHQ criticized the ISC for being made up of parliamentarians: "If it was up to me, frankly, I would have more lay people on it. You might have to make them peers in order to put them on it; but provided they had actually earned public trust in some other field—like journalism, the law, or one or more of the major religions, that would be, I would have thought, fine."[18] Thus, former practitioners have indicated that it would be viable, in principle, for lay people to participate in formal reporting processes. They clearly perceive a need for the public to be seen to have an input into intelligence policy—more directly than ministerial or parliamentary representation can provide.

When it comes to task-oriented accountability, it is apparent that there are already many fruitful exchanges within the agencies, as well as between GCHQ and the NSA, and the Security Service and foreign counterparts, about the use of technology and tradecraft. There are also numerous ad hoc reviews and red teams challenging assumptions, as well as "lessons learned" exercises. This could possibly be enhanced by introducing a more consistent process of peer review with external agencies. The logical forum for this activity would be within the "Five Eyes" network. As discussed earlier, the Security Service has made use of Australian expertise to monitor their performance and provide feedback. This kind of scrutiny could be extended to the other agencies and even the National Security Council and its secretariat, to share best practices. U.K. officials have provided advice to other states on the workings of this forum.[19] It should be feasible to adopt a more established reciprocal arrangement with regular interchange of expertise—subject to the consent of the other members of the network. The advantage of such peer review for the United Kingdom would be that it would gain an insight into the inner operations of its peers, allowing it to learn as well as affording better warning in the future if any of its allies subvert international law or act against U.K. values.

In relation to vernacular accountability, existing formal scrutiny bodies like IPCO have tried to get a sense of the culture of the intelligence and security services, via inspections, interviews, and monitoring of warrant applications and training. This provides a good level of informed oversight, but has little public input. Private firms and civil society groups are also canvassed for their expertise, either on technical matters for the former or on issues like diversity with the latter, but these consultations generally relate to policy more than operational choices. It is always tempting for an academic to suggest a more open discourse between intelligence officials and the general public, but the demands of secrecy present a real challenge for any such proposal—particularly where this might involve actual dialogue rather than simply public speeches by representatives of the national intelligence machinery. The risk of revealing intelligence-gathering techniques or knowledge, and so losing informational advantage, is real. In order to preserve the free exchange of opinion, it may be necessary to accept that some aspects of vernacular accountability have to be undertaken in secret.

That said, far more information could be put into the public domain: on ethics training, the role and nature of staff and ethics counsellors, and the existing forums for staff discussion. Indeed, the staff counsellor could have a more public role, managing queries from wider associated staff or actors linked to the national intelligence machinery, rather than just officials in the three intelligence and security agencies. It is strange that for much of their early history, there was an apparent reluctance for the staff counsellor, members of the IPT, the ISC, and the commissioners to speak to each other and share information and expertise. One important and potentially useful way of expanding vernacular accountability would be for the formal accounting bodies also to engage in these kinds of conversations on a regular basis.

Overall, the lesson of this research is that there is more to intelligence accountability in the United Kingdom than just the formal mechanisms of reporting and oversight. What keeps officials honest and effective are the nature of the task and the everyday interactions between staff, interpreting and enacting intersubjective understandings of what intelligence practice should entail. Generational changes have brought about a vernacular form of accountability, where officials challenge their superiors and question the ethics of policy among themselves. The question for the future is whether this, in combination with formal accountability structures, can manage and limit the momentum toward increased surveillance and governmental intrusion in the name of efficacy and task-oriented accountability, which technology tends to favor. In this sense, the three forms of accountability may coexist and complement each other in many ways—but they also conflict, with important implications for governance and democracy.

Notes

Introduction

1. Gadher, Dipesh, "MI5 Saw London Bridge Killers Set Off in Van," *Sunday Times*, February 18, 2018, 10.

2. Former independent reviewer of terrorism legislation, 2011–17.

3. Anderson, David, *Attacks in London and Manchester March–June 2017: Independent Assessment of MI5 and Police Internal Reviews*. December 2017.

4. ISC, *The 2017 Attacks: What Needs to Change? Westminster, Manchester Arena, London Bridge, Finsbury Park, Parsons Green*. HC1694. London: The Stationery Office, 2018.

5. Anderson, *Attacks*, 27.

6. Ibid., 47.

7. Ibid., 48.

8. Algar, Clare, "The Intelligence and Security Committee: the Government's White-Washing Body of Choice," *New Statesman*, December 19, 2013.

9. Even the ISC's recent report, *Detainee Mistreatment and Rendition: 2001–2010* (London: Stationery Office, 2018), which contained significant criticisms of the agencies, noted: "We do not deny that it is easy to criticize with the benefit of hindsight, and do not seek to blame individual officers acting under immense pressure," 5.

10. Leigh, David, and Richard Norton-Taylor, "How MI5 kept watchdog in the dark over detainees' claims of torture," *Guardian*, February 15, 2010;

Verkaik, Robert, "Former minister: I misled MPs over hooding of prisoners in Iraq," *Independent*, June 3, 2010; Raphael, Sam and Ruth Blakeley, "The stain of Britain's part in torture and rendition will never wash away," *Conversation*, June 29, 2018.

11. Jenkins, Sir Simon, "Edward Snowden has started a global debate. So why the silence in Britain?" *Guardian*, September 19, 2013; Jenkins, Sir Simon, "These fear factory speeches are utterly self-defeating," *Guardian*, November 7, 2007; Milne, Seamus, "A pointless attack on liberty that fuels the terror threat," *Guardian,* November 8, 2007.

12. Gill, Peter, "Security Intelligence and Human Rights: Illuminating the 'Heart of Darkness'?" *Intelligence and National Security*, vol. 24, no. 1 (2009), 79. Loch Johnson has divided contributors to debates over intelligence into four camps: "ostriches," who avoid scrutinizing intelligence activities; "cheerleaders," who sing praises of the agencies; "lemon suckers," perennial critics who see little value in covert action; and "guardians," who are able to offer a detached assessment. See Johnson, Loch K., "The Church Committee Investigation of 1975 and the Evolution of Modern Intelligence Accountability," *Intelligence and National Security*, vol. 23, no. 2 (2008), 199. In the United Kingdom, the general public are often assumed to be ostriches, with the debate left to cheerleaders and lemon suckers.

13. Intelligence is defined in a variety of ways, and can refer to organizations, processes, and the information gathered. For the purpose of this text, I adapt Michael Warner's formulation and see intelligence practice as "secret state activity to understand or influence foreign entities and counter national security threats," adding "national security threats" to acknowledge that intelligence activity is increasingly directed toward domestic as well as foreign actors. Warner, Michael, "Wanted: A Definition of 'Intelligence,'" *Studies in Intelligence*, vol. 46, no. 3, (2002), 15–22. Intelligence, as the product of this activity, is information designed to advantage policymakers in their decisions.

14. Parker, A., "Remarks at a Speech in Central London," October 17, 2017.

15. As the ISC put it in its annual report for 2007–08: "We remain concerned that aspects of the Agencies' work that are not related to international counterterrorism are continuing to suffer as a result of the focus on counterterrorism." (London: Stationery Office, 2008), 28. See also *ISC Annual Report, 2008–09* (London: Stationery Office, 2009), 15.

16. Dearden, Lizzie, "British Police to Investigate Potential Russian State Involvement in Up to 14 Deaths in U.K.," *Independent*, March 13, 2018.

17. Allen, Duncan, "Managed Confrontation: U.K. Policy Towards Russia after the Salisbury Attack," Chatham House Research Paper, October 2018, 2.

18. Although the ISC did question agency heads about the Arab Spring, there was no discussion of whether they had anticipated the rise of Islamic State or retrospective analysis of the intelligence operation in Helmand prior to British

deployment, whether it was sufficient, and whether warnings about the threat environment were heeded among policymakers and the military.

19. In 2006, a raid at an address in Forest Gate, based on faulty intelligence, led to one of the suspects, Abdul Kahar, being accidentally shot and injured. Jean Charles de Menezes, a Brazilian visitor to the United Kingdom, was shot dead on the metro in July 2005 by counterterrorism officers who mistook him for a suicide bomber. The false identification was set in motion by problems with the surveillance team.

20. Burnton, Sir Stanley, *Report of the Interception of Communications Commissioner Annual Report for 2016 (covering the period January to December 2016)*, HC 297 (London: Stationery Office, 2017), 21. The annex to this report details a number of cases of wrongful arrest in that year.

21. Omand, David, *Securing the State* (London: Hurst, 2010).

22. Glees, Anthony, and Philip H. J. Davies, "Intelligence, Iraq, and the Limits of Legislative Accountability During Political Crisis," *Intelligence and National Security*, vol. 21, no. 5 (2006), 858.

23. Qurashi, Fahid, "Prevent Gives People Permission to Hate Muslims—It Has no Place in Schools," *Guardian*, April 4, 2016.

24. Foley, Frank, "The Expansion of Intelligence Agency Mandates: British Counterterrorism in Comparative Perspective," *Review of International Studies*, vol. 35, no. 4 (October 2009), 983–95.

25. Leigh, Ian, "More Closely Watching the Spies: Three Decades of Experiences," in Born, Hans, Loch K. Johnson, and Ian Leigh, *Who's Watching the Spies? Establishing Intelligence Service Accountability* (Washington, D.C.: Potomac Books, 2005), 7; Bruneau, Thomas C., and Steven C. Boraz, "Intelligence Reform: Balancing Democracy and Effectiveness," in Bruneau, Thomas C., and Steven C. Boraz, *Reforming Intelligence* (University of Texas Press, 2007), 5.

26. Merton, Robert K., "Bureaucratic Structure and Personality," in *Social Theory and Social Structure*, edited by Robert K. Merton (Glencoe, Ill.: Free Press, 1957), 195–206; Hannan, M. T., and J. M. Freeman, "Structural Inertia and Organizational Change," *American Sociological Review*, vol. 49, no. 2 (1984), 149–64.

27. Rascoff, Samuel, "Domesticating Intelligence," *Southern California Law Review*, vol. 83 (2010), 581.

28. Foley, Frank, "Why Interagency Operations Break Down: U.S. Counterterrorism in Comparative Perspective," *European Journal of International Security*, vol. 1 (2016), 150–75; Zegart, Amy, *Spying Blind: The CIA, the FBI, and the Origins of 9/11* (Princeton University Press, 2007).

29. Omand, David, and Mark Phythian, *Principled Spying: The Ethics of Secret Intelligence* (Oxford University Press, 2018); Mill, J. S., *On Liberty* (Kitchener: Batoche Books, 2001), 19–20.

30. Gill, P., "Security Intelligence and Human Rights," 90.

31. Andrew, Christopher, *The Defence of the Realm: The Authorised History of MI5* (London: Penguin, 2009); Jeffery, Keith, *The Secret History of MI6* (London: Penguin, 2010); Aldrich, Richard, and Rory Cormac, *The Black Door* (London: William Collins, 2017); Moran, Christopher, *Classified: Secrecy and the Modern State* (Cambridge University Press, 2013).

32. Aldrich, Richard, *GCHQ* (London: HarperCollins, 2011). Correra, Gordon, *MI6* (London: Weidenfeld and Nicolson, 2011).

33. Hewitt, Steve, *The British War on Terror* (London: Continuum, 2008); Foley, Frank, *Countering Terrorism in Britain and France: Institutions, Norms, and the Shadow of the Past* (Cambridge University Press, 2013); Glees, Anthony, and Philip Davies, *Spinning the Spies: Intelligence, Open Government, and the Hutton Inquiry* (London: Social Affairs Unit, 2004).

34. Glees, Anthony, Philip Davies, and John Morrison, *The Open Side of Secrecy: Britain's Intelligence and Security Committee* (London: Social Affairs Unit, 2006); Phythian, Mark, " 'A Very British Institution': The Intelligence and Security Committee and Intelligence Accountability in the United Kingdom," in *Oxford Handbook of National Security Intelligence*, edited by Loch K. Johnson, (Oxford University Press, 2010), 699–718.

35. Omand, *Securing the State*. Omand and Phythian, *Principled Spying*.

36. For a detailed history of GCHQ, see Aldrich, *GCHQ*.

37. The role of special forces is seen as a particularly challenging subject for inquiry, due to the levels of secrecy in operation. See Cormac, Rory, *Disrupt and Deny: Spies, Special Forces, and the Secret Pursuit of British Foreign Policy* (Oxford University Press, 2018); Knowles, Emily, and Abigail Watson, "All Quiet on the ISIS Front: British Secret Warfare in the Information Age," http://remotecontrolproject.org/publications/quiet-isis-front-british-secret-warfare-information-age/; Walpole, Liam, "Out from the Shadows: The Case for External Oversight of U.K. Special Forces," http://www.democraticaudit.com/2018/06/04/out-from-the-shadows-the-case-for-external-oversight-of-uk-special-forces/.

38. *ISC Annual Report, 2003–04* (London: Stationery Office, 2004), 14.

39. For example, the Reith lectures of Eliza Manningham-Buller (former director general of the Security Service), https://www.bbc.co.uk/programmes/p00k0jxm.

40. *Who's Who* entries were a useful source of contact information, along with personal links and academic affiliations.

41. The exception being Margaret Beckett, who was the only foreign secretary cited and happy to be on the record.

42. Hay, Colin, "Interpreting Interpretivism Interpreting Interpretations: The New Hermeneutics of Public Administration," *Public Administration*, vol. 89, no. 1 (2011), 168; Bevir, M., and R. A. W. Rhodes, *Interpreting British Governance* (London: Routledge, 2003).

43. Gadamer, Hans-G., *Truth and Method* (London: Sheed and Ward, 1996), 164–69.

44. Chalmers, Alan F., *What Is This Thing Called Science?* 3rd ed. (London: Hackett, 1999), 39; Gadamer, H.-G., *Truth and Method*, 242–64.

45. Hopf, Ted, *Social Construction of International Politics* (Cornell University Press, 2002), 23.

46. Ibid., 24.

47. These criticisms were also made by the scrutiny bodies themselves, for example, ISC, *Privacy and Security: A Modern and Transparent Legal Framework* (London: Stationery Office, 2015), 2.

48. *ISC Annual Report, 2012–13*, HC547 (London: Stationery Office, 2013), 46.

49. *ISC Annual Report, 2008–09*, Cm7807 (London: Stationery Office, 2009), 11.

50. *ISC Annual Report, 2010–11* (London: Stationery Office, 2011), 72.

51 ISC, *Report on the Intelligence Relating to the Murder of Fusilier Lee Rigby* (London: Stationery Office, 2014), 4.

52. ISC, *Foreign Involvement in the Critical National Infrastructure: The Implications for National Security* (London: Stationery Office, 2013), 20.

53. ISC, *Women in the Intelligence Community* (London: Stationery Office, 2015), 9.

54. Algar, "The Intelligence and Security Committee." For a taste of the criticisms, see the Westminster Hall debate "Intelligence and Security Services," October 31, 2013. http://www.publications.parliament.uk/pa/cm201314/cmhansrd/cm131031/halltext/131031h0001.htm.

55. Hillebrand, Claudia, "The Role of News Media in Intelligence Oversight," *Intelligence and National Security*, vol. 27, no. 5 (2012), 691.

56. Final decisions on membership and the chair have also been taken away from the prime minister, and the committee can now require information rather than just request it. See ISC, *Privacy and Security: A Modern and Transparent Legal Framework*, HC1075, March 12, 2015.

57. https://parliamentsandlegislatures.wordpress.com/2018/01/10/intelligence-security-committee/.

58. Former member of the ISC. Interview with the author.

59. Algar, "The Intelligence and Security Committee."

60. Rifkind, Sir Malcolm, "Intelligence Agencies Should 'Operate in Secret,'" *Telegraph*, October 9, 2013. The ISC and Sir Malcolm were keen to refute the allegation that the agencies were using the PRISM program and their partnership with the NSA to circumvent the warrant process in the United Kingdom. However, there were legal issues over the appropriateness of bulk data capture under the existing regime, which were only resolved in 2014.

61. Algar, "The Intelligence and Security Committee."

62. Glees, Anthony, and Philip H. J. Davies, "Intelligence, Iraq, and the Limits of Legislative Accountability during Political Crisis," *Intelligence and National Security*, vol. 21, no. 5 (2006), 855.

63. Interview with the author.

64. Phythian, M., " 'A Very British Institution', 713.

65. https://www.bbc.co.uk/news/uk-politics-24491443.

66. ISC, *Detainees*; ISC, *What Needs to Change?*

67. Part III powers under RIPA relate to the investigation of electronic data protected by encryption. Section 7 of the Intelligence Services Act relates to acts carried out abroad that would be illegal at home. These are authorized by the secretary of state.

68. https://www.gov.uk/government/organisations/office-of-surveillance-com missioners.

69. Other relevant oversight commissioners include the biometrics commissioner and the surveillance camera commissioner.

70. For example, in May 2016, it ruled that the Foreign and Commonwealth Office was not obliged to reveal the guidance it provided to its personnel on the "passing of intelligence relating to individuals who are at risk of targeted lethal strikes outside traditional battlefields," https://ico.org.uk/media/action-weve-taken/decision-notices/2016/1624286/fs_50599866.pdf.

71. OSC, *Annual Report 2-13-14*, HC 343 (London: Stationery Office, 2014), 10.

72. Ibid.

73. ISComm, *Report of the Intelligence Services Commissioner for 2014*, HC225 (London: Stationery Office, 2015), 40.

74. Ibid.

75. The commissioner noted in 2014 that the current system of authorization "would require dishonesty on the part of more than one person, including a person of some seniority, for such a situation to take place without discovery." That said, they also acknowledged that "the Interception of Communications commissioner disclosed that a GCHQ employee deliberately undertook a number of unauthorized searches." ISComm, *Report of the Intelligence Services Commissioner for 2014* (London: Stationery Office, 2015), 44–45.

76. ISC, *Interim Annual Report, 2000–01* (London: Stationery Office, 2001), 6.

77. *ISC Annual Report, 2010–11* (London: Stationery Office, 2011), 4.

78. Anderson, D., *A Question of Trust: Report of the Investigatory Powers Review* (London: Stationery Office, 2015), 120.

79. Ibid., 122.

80. Ibid.

81. Ibid., 238.

82. Weaver, M., "MI5 Resisting Independent Oversight of Bulk Data Collection," *Guardian*, July 26, 2016.

83. Travis, A., "U.K. Security Agencies Unlawfully Collected Data for 17 Years, Court Rules," *Guardian*, October 17, 2016.

84. Anderson, *A Question of Trust*; RUSI, *Privacy and Security: A Modern and*

Transparent Legal Framework (London: Stationery Office, 2015); Independent Surveillance Review, *A Democratic License to Operate* (London: RUSI, 2015).

85. Draft Investigatory Powers Bill, 8.

86 Written evidence, Dr. Tom Hickman, Blackstone Chambers, April 19, 2016. See also Leigh, "More closely watching the spies," 7.

87. https://assets.publishing.service.gov.uk/government/uploads/system/uploads/attachment_data/file/62632/Consolidated_Guidance_November_2011.pdf.

Chapter 1

1. Messner, M., "The Limits of Accountability," *Accounting, Organizations, and Society*, vol. 34, no. 8 (November 2009), 918–38.

2. Bovens, Mark, Thomas Schillemans, and Robert E. Goodin, "Public Accountability," in Bovens, Goodin, and Schillemans, *Oxford Handbook of Public Accountability* (Oxford University Press, 2014), 3.

3. Bovens, Mark, "Two Concepts of Accountability: Accountability as a Virtue and as a Mechanism," *West European Politics*, vol. 33, no. 5 (2010), 946–67.

4. Bovens, Schillemans, and Goodin, "Public Accountability," 5.

5. Perrin, Burt, Marie-Louise Bemelmans-Videc, and Jeremy Lonsdale, "How Evaluation and Auditing Can Help Bring Accountability into the Twenty-First Century," in Bemelmans-Videc, Lonsdale, and Perrin, *Making Accountability Work* (London: Transaction, 2007), 241.

6. Leigh, Ian, "More Closely Watching the Spies: Three Decades of Experiences," in Born, Hans, Loch K. Johnson, and Ian Leigh, *Who's Watching the Spies? Establishing Intelligence Service Accountability* (Washington, D.C.: Potomac Books, 2005).

7. Moran, Christopher, *Classified: Secrecy and the Modern State* (Cambridge University Press, 2013).

8. Hughes, Owen E., *Public Management and Administration: An Introduction* (Basingstoke, U.K.: Palgrave, 2003), 243.

9. Romzek, Barbara S., and Melvin J. Dubnick, "Accountability in the Public Sector: Lessons from the *Challenger* Tragedy," *Public Administration Review*, vol. 47, no. 3 (1987), 227–38.

10. Behn, Robert D., *Rethinking Democratic Accountability* (Brookings, 2001).

11. Kroon, Marceline B. R., Paul t'Hart, and Dik van Kreveld, "Managing Group Decision Making Processes: Individual Versus Collective Accountability and Groupthink," *International Journal of Conflict Management*, vol. 2, no. 2 (1991), 91–115.

12. Bovens, Schillemans, and Goodin, "Public Accountability," 10.

13. ISC, *Detainee Mistreatment and Rendition: 2001–2010* (London: Stationery Office, 2018), 10.

14. Leigh, Ian, "Changing the Rules of the Game: Some Necessary Legal

Reforms to United Kingdom Intelligence," *Review of International Studies*, vol. 35, no. 4 (October 2009), 954; Leigh, Ian, "Intelligence and the Law in the United Kingdom," in *Oxford Handbook of National Security Intelligence*, edited by Loch K. Johnson (Oxford University Press, 2010), 643–44.

15. Grant, Ruth, and Robert. O. Keohane, "Accountability and Abuses of Power in World Politics," *American Political Science Review*, vol. 99, no. 1 (February 2005), 32.

16. Caparini, Marina, "Controlling and Overseeing Intelligence Services in Democratic States," in Hans Born and Marina Caparini, *Democratic Control of Intelligence Services* (London: Ashgate, 2007), 9.

17. Aldrich, Richard. J., and Christopher. Moran, "Delayed Disclosure: National Security, Whistleblowers, and the Nature of Secrecy," *Political Studies*, vol. 67, no. 2 (2019), 1–16.

18. National Commission on Terrorist Attacks, *The 9/11 Commission Report* (Washington, D.C.: National Commission on Terrorist Attacks, 2004).

19. Younger, Alex, "Remarks by the Chief of the Secret Intelligence Service." Vauxhall Cross, December 8, 2016, https://www.sis.gov.uk/news/inside-the-modern-day-mi6.html.

20. Aldrich, Richard J., and Daniela Richterova, "Ambient Accountability: Intelligence Services in Europe and the Decline of State Secrecy," *West European Politics*, vol. 41, no. 4 (2018), 1003.

21. Ibid., 2.

22. Aldrich and Moran, "Delayed Disclosure," 12.

23. Gill, Peter, "The Intelligence and Security Committee and the Challenge of Security Networks," *Review of International Studies*, vol. 35, no. 4 (October 2009), 932.

24. Gill, Peter, "Security Intelligence and Human Rights: Illuminating the 'Heart of Darkness'?" *Intelligence and National Security*, vol. 24, no. 1 (2009), 99.

25. As of 2017, SIS had a total staff of 3,289; GCHQ, 5,988; Security Service, 4,058; Defence Intelligence, 3,876; and the National Security Secretariat, 120; see *ISC Annual Report, 2017–18* (London: Stationery Office, 2018), 15–18.

26. Owen, Paul, "Spy agency chiefs defend surveillance—as it happened," *Guardian*, November 7, 2013.

27. http://www.publications.parliament.uk/pa/ld200405/ldjudgmt/jd041216/a&oth-2.htm; see also Elliott, M., "United Kingdom: The 'War on Terror,' U.K.-style—The Detention and Deportation of Suspected Terrorists," *International Journal of Constitutional Law*, vol. 8, no. 1 (2010), 131–45.

28. https://www.echr.coe.int/Documents/FS_Mass_surveillance_ENG.pdf.

29. For an entertaining exploration of how the law is crowding out political space in the United Kingdom, see Jonathan Sumption's 2019 Reith Lectures: https://www.bbc.co.uk/programmes/m00057m8.

30. IPCO, *Approval of Warrants, Authorizations, and Notices by Judicial Commissioners*, Advisory Notice 1/2018, March 8, 2018.

31. ISC, *Privacy and Security: A Modern and Transparent Legal Framework* (London: Stationery Office, 2015), 66.

32. Edgar, Timothy H., *Beyond Snowden: Privacy, Mass Surveillance, and the Struggle to Reform the NSA* (Brookings, 2017).

33. In fact, bulk data capture is not contrary to FISA; see Edgar, Timothy, "Bulk NSA Internet Program Shows the Complete Incoherence of Surveillance Law," https://www.lawfareblog.com/bulk-nsa-internet-program-shows-complete-incoherence-surveillance-law.

34. McCubbins, Mathew D., and Thomas Schwartz, "Congressional Oversight Overlooked: Police Patrols versus Fire Alarms," *American Journal of Political Science*, vol. 28, no. 1 (February 1984), 165–79; Johnson, Loch K., "Accountability and America's Secret Foreign Policy: Keeping a Legislative Eye on the Central Intelligence Agency," *Foreign Policy Analysis*, vol. 1 (2005), 100–01.

35. Aldrich, Richard J., "Global Intelligence Cooperation versus Accountability: New Facets to an Old Problem," *Intelligence and National Security*, vol. 24, no. 1 (2009), 36. Despite these criticisms, Frank Foley has asserted that "when compared to the French case at least, the political accountability of the British intelligence agencies appears relatively high." See Foley, Frank, "The Expansion of Intelligence Agency Mandates: British Counterterrorism in Comparative Perspective," *Review of International Studies*, vol. 35, no. 4 (October 2009), 995.

36. Wills, Aidan, and Hans Born, "International Intelligence Cooperation and Accountability: Formidable Challenges and Imperfect Solutions," in *International Intelligence Cooperation and Accountability*, edited by Hans Born, Ian Leigh, and Aidan Wills (London: Routledge, 2011), 279. Iain Cameron cites a constitutional lawyer, Dawn Oliver, who defined accountability as "being liable to be required to give an account or explanation of actions and, where appropriate, to suffer the consequences, take the blame, or undertake to put matters right." Cameron, Iain, "Beyond the Nation State: The Influence of the European Court of Human Rights on Intelligence Accountability," in *International Intelligence Cooperation and Accountability*, edited by Born, Leigh, and Wills, 37. The idea of "suffering" and "blame" seems to identify accountability strongly with punishment here.

37. Hastedt, Glenn, "The Politics of Intelligence Accountability," in *Oxford Handbook of National Security Intelligence*, 720–21.

38. http://www.legislation.gov.uk/ukpga/2016/25/section/25/enacted#section-25-3.

39. Leppard, David, "MI6 'Forced Straw to Admit' He Approved Suspect's Rendition," *Sunday Times*, April 15, 2012.

40. Aftergood, Steven, "Reducing Government Secrecy: Finding What Works," *Yale Law and Policy Review*, vol. 27, no. 2 (2009), 399.

41. Andregg, Michael, "Ethics and Professional Intelligence," in *Oxford Handbook of National Security Intelligence*, 748.

42. Foley, Frank, "Why Inter-Agency Operations Break Down: U.S. Counterterrorism in Comparative Perspective," *European Journal of International Security*, vol. 1 (2016), 150–75; Zegart, Amy, *Spying Blind: The CIA, the FBI, and the Origins of 9/11* (Princeton University Press, 2007).

43. Weiner, Tim, *Legacy of Ashes* (London: Penguin, 2008), 119.

44. Ibid.

45. Cobain, Ian, *Cruel Britannia* (London: Portobello Books, 2012), 161, 168.

46. Betts, Richard, *The Enemies of Intelligence: Knowledge and Power in American National Security* (Columbia University Press, 2007), 9–10.

47. Keefer, Philip, and Steven Knack, "Boondoggles, Rent-Seeking, and Political Checks and Balances: Public Investment under Unaccountable Governments," *Review of Economics and Statistics*, vol. 89, no. 3 (2007), 566–72.

48. Pincher, C., *Traitors: The Labyrinths of Treason* (London: Sidgwick & Jackson, 1987). For an account of alleged coup plotting in the United Kingdom, see Aldrich, R., and R. Cormac, *The Black Door* (London: William Collins, 2017), 318–28.

49. Rimington, Stella, *Open Secret* (London: Hutchinson, 2001), 117–18. For similar problems in the U.S. context, see Christensen, Tom, and others, *Organization Theory and the Public Sector* (London: Routledge, 2007), 52–54.

50. Former cabinet secretary. Interview with the author. The Cambridge spy ring was a group of British Cambridge graduates (five of whom—Anthony Blunt, Kim Philby, Guy Burgess, Donald Maclean, and probably Jonathan Cairncross—became notorious as the Cambridge Five), who passed secrets to the Soviet Union from the 1930s to the 1950s. Blunt worked for MI5 during the war, Philby for MI6, Burgess and Maclean were diplomats, and Cairncross worked for the Cabinet Office, Government Code, and Cypher School (the forerunner of GCHQ) at Bletchley Park, as well as MI6.

51. Former senior SIS officer. Interview with the author.

52. Tetlock, Philip E., and Barbara A. Mellers, "Intelligent Management of Intelligence Agencies: Beyond Accountability Ping-Pong," *American Psychologist* (September 2011), 543–44. On the dangers of excessive accountability, see Flinders, Matthew, "Daring to be a Daniel: The Pathology of Politicized Accountability in a Monitory Democracy," *Administration & Society*, vol. 43, no. 5 (2011), 595–619.

53. Omand, David, and Mark Phythian, *Principled Spying: The Ethics of Secret Intelligence* (Oxford University Press, 2018); *Ethics of Spying*, edited by Jan Goldman (Plymouth: Scarecrow Press, 2010); Macintyre, Ben, *A Spy Among Friends* (London: Bloomsbury, 2015), especially the Afterword.

54. Moran, *Classified*, 344.

55. Cameron, David. *For the Record* (London: William Collins, 2019), 452.

56. The intended targets being Gamal Nasser, president of Egypt, and Idi

Amin, president of Uganda; see Aldrich, Richard, and Rory Cormac, *The Black Door* (London: William Collins, 2017), 202.

57. Aldrich and Cormac, *The Black Door*, 261.

58. Ibid., 260–61.

59. Merton, Robert K., "Bureaucratic Structure and Personality," *Social Forces*, vol. 18, no. 4 (May 1940), 560–68; Hannan, Michael T., and John M. Freeman, "Structural Inertia and Organizational Change," *American Sociological Review*, vol. 49, no. 2 (1984), 149–64; Rascoff, Sam, "Domesticating intelligence," *Southern California Law Review*, vol. 83 (2010), 581.

60. The benefits to public organizations from openness and transparency have been affirmed repeatedly by the U.K. government's national action plans for open government and open policymaking. The latest iteration is the *U.K. National Action Plan for Open Government 2019–21*, https://www.gov.uk/government/publications/uk-national-action-plan-for-open-government-2019-2021/uk-national-action-plan-for-open-government-2019-2021#introduction.

61. Chilcot, Sir John. *Report of the Iraq Inquiry: Executive Summary* (London: Stationery Office, 2016), 45.

62. https://www.un.org/press/en/2003/sc7682.doc.htm.

63. For a critique of Rascoff's prescriptions, see Berman, Emily, "Regulating Domestic Intelligence Collection," *Washington and Lee Law Review*, vol. 71, no. 1 (2014), 78–79.

64. Edmunds, Timothy, "British Civil-Military Relations and the Problem of Risk," *International Affairs*, vol. 88, no. 2 (March 2012), 272.

65. European Commission for Democracy Through Law (Venice Commission), *Update of the 2007 Report*, http://www.venice.coe.int/webforms/documents/default.aspx?pdffile=CDL-AD(2015)006-e.

66. Lunn, Simon, "The Democratic Control of Armed Forces in Principle and Practice," in Born, Hans, Philipp Fluri, and Simon Lunn, *Oversight and Guidance*. DCAF, Geneva, 2010, 28.

67. Simon, Jonathan, "Parrhesiastic Accountability: Investigatory Commissions and Executive Power in an Age of Terror," *Yale Law Journal* (2005), 1432.

68. Johnson, Loch K., "Accountability and America's Secret Foreign Policy: Keeping a Legislative Eye on the Central Intelligence Agency," *Foreign Policy Analysis*, vol. 1 (2005), 100.

69. Omand and Phythian, *Principled Spying*, 217.

70. Bruneau, Thomas C., and Steven C. Boraz, "Best Practices: Balancing Democracy and Effectiveness," in *Reforming Intelligence: Obstacles to Democratic Control and Effectiveness*, edited by T. C. Bruneau and S. C. Boraz (University of Texas Press, 2007), 338; Matei, Florina C., "The Media's Role in Intelligence Democratization," *International Journal of Intelligence and Counterintelligence*, vol. 27, no. 1 (2014), 76.

71. March, James G., and Johan P. Olsen, "The Logic of Appropriateness," in

Oxford Handbook of Public Policy, edited by Michael Moran, Martin Rein, and Robert E. Goodin (Oxford University Press, 2006), 689–708.

72. European Commission for Democracy Through Law (Venice Commission), *Report on the Democratic Oversight of the Security Service* (Strasbourg: Council of Europe, 2015), 17–18.

73. Beutler, Brian, "The Benghazi Witch-Hunt Against Hillary Is Backfiring Just Like Bill Clinton's Impeachment," *New Republic*, October 19, 2015. See also Betts, Richard, *Enemies of Intelligence: Knowledge and Power in American National Security* (Columbia University Press, 2009), 66–103.

74. Glees, Anthony, and Philip H. J. Davies, *Spinning the Spies: Intelligence, Open Government, and the Hutton Inquiry* (London: Social Affairs Unit, 2004).

75. Hillebrand, Claudia, "The Role of News Media in Intelligence Oversight," *Intelligence and National Security*, vol. 27, no. 5 (2012), 693.

76. Ibid., 697.

77. Ibid., 699.

78. https://www.itv.com/news/update/2014-01-28/gchq-we-do-not-comment-of-intelligence-matters/.

79. Aldrich and Cormac, *The Black Door*, 186.

80. Wilkinson, Nicholas, *Secrecy and the Media: The Official History of the United Kingdom's D-Notice System* (London: Routledge, 2009).

81. https://www.theguardian.com/media/2015/jul/31/d-notice-system-state-media-press-freedom.

82. Barber, Stephen, "Can Parliamentary Oversight of Security and Intelligence Be Considered More Open Government Than Accountability?" *International Public Management Review*, vol. 18, no. 1 (2017), 47–48.

83. White, Gregory, "This Is the Wikileak that Sparked the Tunisian Crisis," *Business Insider*, January 14, 2011.

84. https://disinformationreport.blob.core.windows.net/disinformation-report/NewKnowledge-Disinformation-Report-Whitepaper-121718.pdf; https://comprop.oii.ox.ac.uk/wp-content/uploads/sites/93/2018/12/IRA-Report-2018.pdf.

85. Parker, Andrew, "Speech to BfV Symposium," May 14, 2018. https://www.mi5.gov.uk/news/director-general-andrew-parker-speech-to-bfv-symposium.

86. Parker, Andrew, "MI5 Chief Security Speech," RUSI, Whitehall, October 8, 2013. https://www.telegraph.co.uk/news/uknews/defence/10366119/MI5-chief-security-speech.html.

87. Parker, A., "Speech to BfV Symposium."

88. Younger, Alex, "Fourth Generation Espionage—Fusing Traditional Human Skills With Innovation," December 3, 2018. https://www.sis.gov.uk/news/alex-younger-st-andrews-speech.html; Lobban, Iain, "GCHQ and Turing's Legacy," University of Leeds, October 4, 2012. https://www.gchq.gov.uk/speech/director-gchq-makes-speech-tribute-alan-turing.

89. Younger, Alex, "Inside the Modern-Day MI6," Vauxhall Cross, December 8, 2016. https://www.sis.gov.uk/news/inside-the-modern-day-mi6.html.

90. Hannigan, Robert, "Director GCHQ's Speech at Stonewall Workplace Conference," April 15, 2016. https://www.gchq.gov.uk/speech/director-gchqs-speech-stonewall-workplace-conference-delivered.

91. Sengupta, Kim, "Rights and Wrongs of Rendition: MI5 Consults 'Ethical Counselor,'" *Independent*, March 6, 2009.

92. Caparini, "Controlling and Overseeing Intelligence Services in Democratic States," 9.

93. Leigh, Ian, "More Closely Watching the Spies: Three Decades of Experiences," 7.

94. Edmunds, Timothy, "Intelligence Agencies and Democratization: Continuity and Change in Serbia after Milosevic," *Europe-Asia Studies*, vol. 60, no. 1 (January 2008), 25–48.

95. Bruneau, Thomas C., and Steven C. Boraz, "Intelligence Reform: Balancing Democracy and Effectiveness," in Bruneau and Boraz, *Reforming Intelligence*, 5; Matei, "The Media's Role in Intelligence Democratization," 76.

96. Gill, "The Intelligence and Security Committee," 932.

97. Venice Commission, *Report on the Democratic Oversight of the Security Services*, adopted by the Venice Commission at its 71st plenary session (Venice, June 1–2, 2007), 4; Venice Commission, *Update of the 2007 Report on the Democratic Oversight of the Security Services and Report on the Democratic Oversight of Signals Intelligence Agencies*, adopted by the Venice Commission at its 102nd plenary session (Venice, March 20–21, 2015), 9–10; Ian Leigh, "Changing the Rules of the Game: Some Necessary Legal Reforms to United Kingdom Intelligence," *Review of International Studies*, vol. 35, no. 4 (October 2009), 943–55.

98. Lahneman, William J., "U.S. Intelligence Prior to 9/11 and Obstacles to Reform," in Bruneau and Boraz, *Reforming Intelligence*; see also Gill, Peter, "Keeping 'Earthly Awkwardness': Failures of Intelligence in the United Kingdom," in the same volume, 97.

99. Hughes, Owen E., *Public Management and Administration: An Introduction* (Basingstoke, U.K.: Palgrave, 2003), 237.

100. Further ones might operate between the government and individual ministers, or between lower level officials and their line managers.

101. Omand, David, *Securing the State* (London: Hurst, 2010).

102. https://civilservicecommission.independent.gov.uk/wp-content/uploads/2018/09/diplomatic.pdf.

103. Moran, *Classified*; Bruce, James B., Sina Beaghley, and W. George Jameson, "Secrecy in U.S. National Security: Why a Paradigm Shift Is Needed," *Perspective*, November 2018. https://www.rand.org/content/dam/rand/pubs/perspectives/PE300/PE305/RAND_PE305.pdf.

104. European Commission for Democracy Through Law (Venice Commis-

sion), *Report on the Democratic Oversight of the Security Service*, June 11, 2007 (Strasbourg: Council of Europe, 2007), 16–17.

105. Bouckaert, Geert, and John Halligan, *Managing Performance* (London: Routledge, 2008).

106. Omand, *Securing the State*, 265–67; Matei, "The Media's Role in Intelligence Democratization," 85.

107. Donohue, Laura, *The Costs of Counterterrorism* (Cambridge University Press, 2008), 116.

108. Christensen, Tom, and others, *Organization Theory and the Public Sector* (London: Routledge, 2007), 108.

109. Farson, Stuart, and Reg Whitaker, "Accounting for the Future or the Past? Developing Accountability and Oversight Systems to Meet Future Intelligence Needs," in *Oxford Handbook of National Security Intelligence*, 678.

110. Grant and Keohane, "Accountability and Abuses of Power in World Politics," 30.

111. Sejersted, Fredrik, "Intelligence and Accountability in a State without Enemies," in *Who's Watching the Spies?*, 130–31; Roberts, Nancy, "Keeping Public Officials Accountable through Dialogue: Resolving the Accountability Paradox," *Public Administration Review*, vol. 62, no. 6 (November/December 2002), 658–69.

112. Weller, Geoffrey R., "Oversight of Australia's Intelligence Services," *International Journal of Intelligence and Counterintelligence*, vol. 12, no. 4 (1999), 503.

113. Richards, David, and Martin J. Smith, "The Westminster Model and the 'Indivisibility of the Political and Administrative Elite': A Convenient Myth Whose Time Is Up?" *Governance*, vol. 29, no. 4 (2016), 499–516.

114. Bevir, Mark, and David Richards, "Decentring Policy Networks: A Theoretical Agenda," *Public Administration*, vol. 87, no. 1 (2009), 3–14.

115. Aradau, Claudia, and Tobias Blanke, "Governing Others: Anomaly and the Algorithmic Subject of Security," *European Journal of International Security*, vol. 3, no. 1 (February 2018), 1–21.

116. https://www.Chathamhouse.org/sites/default/files/publications/research/2018-06-14-artificial-intelligence-international-affairs-cummings-roff-cukier-parakilas-bryce.pdf, 4.

117. https://www.Chathamhouse.org/sites/default/files/publications/research/2018-06-14-artificial-intelligence-international-affairs-cummings-roff-cukier-parakilas-bryce.pdf, 5.

118. O'Neil, Cathy, *Weapons of Math Destruction: How Big Data Increases Inequality and Threatens Democracy* (London: Penguin, 2016).

119. https://www.accessnow.org/the-toronto-declaration-protecting-the-rights-to-equality-and-non-discrimination-in-machine-learning-systems/.

120. https://www.accessnow.org/the-toronto-declaration-protecting-the-rights-to-equality-and-non-discrimination-in-machine-learning-systems/.

121. IPCO, *Annual Report of the Investigatory Powers Commissioner 2017* (London: Stationery Office, 2019), 8.

122. RUSI, *A Democratic Licence to Operate: Report of the Independent Surveillance Review* (London: RUSI, 2015), 56.

123. RUSI, *A Democratic Licence to Operate*, 56.

124. Hansard, "Staff Counsellor for the Security and Intelligence Agencies: Written Statement—HCWS694," April 21, 2016, https://www.parliament.uk/business/publications/written-questions-answers-statements/written-statement/Commons/2016-04-21/HCWS694/.

125. *U.K. National Intelligence Services Handbook* (Washington, D.C.: International Business Publications, 2013), 116.

126. RUSI, *A Democratic Licence to Operate*, 56.

127. Savage, A., *Leaks, Whistleblowing, and the Public Interest: The Law of Unauthorised Disclosures* (London: Edward Elgar, 2016), 209.

128. Ibid., 207–10.

129. Vega, M. A., "Beyond Incentives: Making Corporate Whistleblowing Moral in the New Era of Dodd-Frank Act 'Bounty Hunting,'" *Connecticut Law Review*, vol. 45, no. 2 (2012), 490.

130. Ibid.

131. Watson, Chanel L., and Tom O'Connor, "Legislating for Advocacy: The Case of Whistleblowing," *Nursing Ethics*, vol. 24, no. 3 (2017), 307.

132. Andrew, Christopher, *The Defence of the Realm: The Authorized History of MI5* (London: Penguin, 2010), 824–26.

133. Zimbardo, Philip, *The Lucifer Effect* (St Ives: Random House, 2007).

134. *Whistleblowing in the Social Services*, edited by G. Hunt (London: Arnold, 1998), 5.

135. Ibid., 5.

136. Ahern, Kathryn, and Sally McDonald, "The Beliefs of Nurses Who Were Involved in a Whistleblowing Event," *Journal of Advanced Nursing*, vol. 38, no. 3 (May 2002), 303–09.

137. Congressional Research Service, *Intelligence Community Whistleblower Protections*, September 23, 2019, https://fas.org/sgp/crs/intel/R45345.pdf.

138. Gopnik, Adam. "Why Is Trump Obsessed with Outing the Whistle-Blower?" *The New Yorker*, November 7, 2019.

139. Ibid.

140. Gill, Peter, "The Intelligence and Security Committee and the Challenge of Security Networks," *Review of International Studies*, vol. 35, no. 4 (October 2009), 937.

Chapter 2

1. ISComm, *Report of the Intelligence Services Commissioner for 2016* (London: Stationery Office, 2017), 5.

2. In 2008, the ISC annual report for 2007–06 noted: "Sir Paul Kennedy, the Interception of Communications commissioner, and Sir Peter Gibson, the Intelligence Services commissioner, took up post in April 2006. The new commissioners have told us that they have been impressed by the integrity and quality of the Agencies' work—particularly by how promptly they report any mistakes." *ISC Annual Report, 2006–07*, Cm7299 (London: Stationery Office, 2008), 27.

3. *ISC Annual Report, 2004–05*, Cm6510 (London: Stationery Office, 2005), 4.

4. Porter, Patrick, *Blunder: Britain's War in Iraq* (Oxford University Press, 2018).

5. Chilcot, Sir John, *Report of the Iraq Inquiry: Executive Summary* (London: Stationery Office, 2016), 45.

6. Chilcot, *Executive Summary*, 76; Blix, Hans, *12th Quarterly Report of UNMOVIC*, http://www.un.org/Depts/unmovic/SC7asdelivered.htm.

7. U.K. government, *Iraq's Weapons of Mass Destruction: The Assessment of the British Government*, https://nsarchive2.gwu.edu/NSAEBB/NSAEBB80/wmd11.pdf.

8. Hutton, Lord, *Report of the Inquiry into the Circumstances Surrounding the Death of Dr. David Kelly C.M.G.* (London: Stationery Office, 2004), 320.

9. Butler, Lord, *Review of Intelligence on Weapons of Mass Destruction* (London: Stationery Office, 2004), 82.

10. Chilcot, Sir John, *The Report of the Iraq Inquiry: Volume IV* (London: Stationery Office, 2016), 65.

11. *ISC Annual Report, 1999–2000* (London: Stationery Office, 2000), 8; *ISC Annual Report, 2001–02* (London: Stationery Office, 2000), 7.

12. Chilcot, *Executive Summary*, 74.

13. U.K. government, *Iraq's Weapons of Mass Destruction*, 4.

14. Chilcot, *Volume IV*, 239–40.

15. Chilcot, *Executive Summary*, 117; *ISC Annual Report, 2004–05*, 22–23.

16. Chilcot, *Executive Summary*. Chilcot argued that Iraq had left a "damaging legacy, which may make it more difficult to secure support for government policy, including military action, where the evidence depends on inferential judgements drawn from intelligence" (116).

17. See Gaskarth, Jamie, "Intervention: Domestic Contestation and Britain's National Role Conceptions" in *Domestic Role Contestation, Foreign Policy, and International Relations*, edited by Cristian Cantir and Juliet Kaarbo (London: Routledge, 2016).

18. Eaton, G., "Jeremy Corbyn's Russia Stance Has Reopened Old Wounds," *New Statesman*, March 14, 2018.

19. *ISC Annual Report, 2005–06* (London: Stationery Office, 2006), 7; *ISC Annual Report, 2008–09* (London: Stationery Office, 2010), 33.

20. *ISC Annual Report, 2004–05*, 26.

21. *ISC Annual Report, 2001–02*, 21.

22. Ibid., 22.

23. Defence Select Committee, *Operations in Afghanistan,* vol. I (London: Stationery Office, 2011), 21–22.

24. Farrell, Theo, "Improving in War: Military Adaptation and the British in Helmand Province, Afghanistan, 2006–09," *Journal of Strategic Studies*, vol. 33, no. 4 (2010), 575, fn30.

25. https://assets.publishing.service.gov.uk/government/uploads/system/uploads/attachment_data/file/503022/20160222_Op_Herrick_Casualty_Tables_Feb_16_REVISION.pdf. As the table indicates, only 2 of the 453 total fatalities were incurred prior to 2006.

26. *ISC Annual Report, 2011–12* (London: Stationery Office, 2012), 13.

27. Ibid., 14.

28. Harris, Shane, "Obama's Islamic State Blame Game," *Foreign Policy*, September 29, 2014; Geertz, Bill, "CIA Blew It in Iraq, Blamed for Failing to Warn about Rise of Islamic State," *Washington Times*, July 1, 2014; Kam, Ephraim, "The Rise of the Islamic State: The Strategic Surprise," *INSS Insight*, no. 615, October 13, 2014.

29. ISC, *U.K. Lethal Drone Strikes in Syria* (London: Stationery Office, 2017).

30. *ISC Annual Report, 2003–04* (London: Stationery Office, 2004), 9–10.

31. Ibid.

32. The Butler report sought to balance failures over Iraq with positive results on these two countries, but, as Richard Aldrich has pointed out, the cases it chose to focus on were selective and the inquiry missed the lack of awareness of Soviet development of chemical and biological weapons in breach of treaty obligations. Aldrich, Richard, *GCHQ* (London: HarperCollins, 2011), 531.

33. Correra, G., *MI6: Life and Death in the British Secret Service* (London: Weidenfeld & Nicolson, 2011), 317.

34. Correra, *MI6*, 336; Cormac, Rory, *Disrupt and Deny: Spies, Special Forces, and the Secret Pursuit of British Foreign Policy* (Oxford University Press, 2018), 251.

35. Butler, *Review of Intelligence.*

36. Chilcot, Sir John, *Report of the Iraq Inquiry,* Volume VII (London: Stationery Office, 2016), 77.

37. Ibid., 541.

38. *Report DOC*, March 17, 2010, "Operation TELIC Lessons Study Vol. 4," as cited in Chilcot, Sir John, *Report of the Iraq Inquiry,* Volume XI (London: Stationery Office, 2016), 217.

39. Defence Select Committee, *Operations in Afghanistan*, vol. I (London: Stationery Office, 2011), 21–22.

40. *ISC Annual Report, 2013–14* (London: Stationery Office, 2014), 13.

41. Former senior SIS officer. Interview with the author.

42. Ibid.

43. Ibid.

44. Former chief, SIS. Interview with the author.

45. ISC, *Report on the Intelligence Relating to the Murder of Fusilier Lee Rigby* (London: Stationery Office, 2014), 126.

46. ISC, *Report on the Intelligence Relating to the Murder*, 52, 126.

47. *ISC Annual Report, 2008–09*, 38; *ISC Annual Report 2016–17* (London: Stationery Office, 2017), HC 655.

48. ISC, *Detainee Mistreatment and Rendition: 2001–10* (London: Stationery Office, 2018), 34.

49. ISC, *Detainee Mistreatment and Rendition*, 77.

50. It was also apparently contrary to the stated policy of SIS at the time. The Gibson inquiry revealed that SIS had provided them with "documents, which show that, from at least 2001, it was its policy to record all substantive information, including relevant operational activity" and that "In April 2002, SIS instructions to officers at Guantanamo suggested that the practice in Afghanistan was to record a detainee's physical and mental condition before beginning each interview." Gibson, Sir Peter, *The Report of the Detainee Inquiry* (London: Stationery Office, 2013), 51.

51. ISC, *Detainee Mistreatment and Rendition*, 68.

52. Ibid., 128.

53. Ibid.

54. *ISC Annual Report, 2006–07*, 27.

55. ISC, *Detainee Mistreatment and Rendition*, 5.

56. Ibid., 61.

57. Ibid., 66.

58. That is not to say that personnel were entirely untrained. In the ISC's 2005 report, the agencies argued that they "regarded the normal level of training, which emphasised the requirements of the Human Rights Act 1998, as sufficient for the staff deploying to Afghanistan." ISC, *The Handling of Detainees by UK Intelligence Personnel in Afghanistan, Guantanamo Bay and Iraq* (London: Stationery Office, 2005), 12.

59. Gill, Peter, "Security Intelligence and Human Rights: Illuminating the 'Heart of Darkness'?," *Intelligence and National Security*, vol. 24, no. 1 (2009), 101.

60. http://news.bbc.co.uk/1/hi/world/europe/4638136.stm.

61. https://www.bbc.co.uk/news/world-europe-16614209.

62. Cormac, *Disrupt and Deny*, 252. Some sources allege this individual was put up to it by the ISI, Pakistan's intelligence service. See https://wondersofpakistan.wordpress.com/2011/11/14/the-grocer-and-alice%E2%80%99s-cat/ and Partlow, Joshua, "Negotiator for Taliban was an impostor, Afghan officials say," *Washington Post*, November 23, 2010.

63. Chulov, Martin, "SAS and MI6 officers released by Libya's rebel commanders," *Guardian*, March 7, 2011.

64. Cormac, Rory, and Oliver J. Daddow, "Covert Action Failure and Fiasco Construction: William Hague's 2011 Libyan Venture," *Journal of European Public Policy*, vol. 25, no. 5 (2017), 690–707.

65. *ISC Annual Report, 2011–12*, 18–19.

66. Ibid., 16.

67. Ibid., 17.

68. U.K. government, *Government Response to the Intelligence and Security Committee's Annual Report 2011–12* (London: Stationery Office, 2012), 7.

69. Ibid., 5.

70. Ibid., 6.

71. *ISC Annual Report, 2011–12*, 55.

72. IOCCO, *Report of the Interception of Communications Commissioner Annual Report for 2016, Annex D: Serious Errors* (London: Stationery Office, 2017).

73. *Report of the Interception of Communications Commissioner, 2016*, 56–58.

74. https://www.bbc.co.uk/news/uk-39328853.

75. Marsden, Sam, Wesley Johnson, and Katie Hodge, "Coroner hits out over MI5 photo at 7/7 inquest," *Independent,* May 6, 2011.

76. Ibid.

77. ISC, *Annual Report, 2010–11* (London: Stationery Office, 2011), 72–73.

78. ISC, *Annual Report, 2007–08* (London: Stationery Office, 2008), 40.

79. The Register, "Security agencies work on Scope II replacement," *Guardian*, March 15, 2010.

80. *ISC Annual Report, 2010–11*, 22.

81. *ISC Annual Report, 2007–08*, 29.

82. Ibid., 12.

83. *ISC Annual Report, 2012–13* (London: Stationery Office, 2013), 4.

84. Ibid, 4.

85. Ibid., 67.

86. *ISC Annual Report, 2010–11*, 35.

87. *ISC Annual Report, 2003–04*, 29; Norton-Taylor, Richard, "Security guard jailed for trying to sell secrets," *Guardian*, February 2, 2002.

88. https://www.bbc.co.uk/news/uk-41415328.

89. Dearden, Lizzie, "Man arrested over suspected plot to pass British military secrets to China," *Independent*, June 14, 2018.

90. https://www.dailymail.co.uk/news/article-5548347/Former-MI5-agent-warns-Putin-ten-steps-ahead.html.

91. Norton-Taylor, Richard, "Official fined for leaving al-Qaida papers on train," *Guardian*, October 29, 2008.

92. *ISC Annual Report, 2007–08* (London: Stationery Office, 2008), 20.

93. Ibid.

94. Omand, David, and Mark Phythian, *Principled Spying: The Ethics of Secret Intelligence* (Oxford University Press, 2018), 222.

95. ISC, *The Handling of Detainees*, 6.

96. Ibid., 14.

97. *The Report of the Detainee Inquiry,* December 2013, 2.

98. Ibid.

99. Ibid., 7.

100. Ibid., 54.

101. The inquiry notes that Jack Straw, the foreign secretary, wrote to David Blunkett, the home secretary, on December 21, 2001, to ask whether an extradition bill could include provisions to allow rendition to the United Kingdom. *The Report of the Detainee Inquiry*, 35.

102. Cobain, Ian, "Libyan Rendition: How U.K.'s Role in Kidnap of Families Came to Light," *Guardian*, May 10, 2018.

103. Ibid.

104. Ibid.

105. Syal, Rajeev, and Ian Cobain, "Jack Straw Faces Call to Give Evidence over Role in Libyan Rendition," *Guardian*, May 11, 2018.

106. https://hansard.parliament.uk/commons/2018-05-10/debates/B9AD50CD-9D54-41DA-A18B-1526E7658593/BelhajAndBoudcharLitigationUpdate.

107. ISC, *Intelligence and Security Committee of Parliament Detainee Mistreatment and Rendition: 2001–2010* (London: Stationery Office, 2018), 3.

108. Evidence to the Human Rights Joint Committee, 26 February 2009, https://publications.parliament.uk/pa/jt200809/jtselect/jtrights/152/15207.htm.

109. Gaskarth, Jamie, "Entangling Alliances? The U.K.'s Complicity in Torture in the Global War on Terror," *International Affairs*, vol. 87, no. 4 (July 2011), 945–64.

110. *Detainee Mistreatment and Rendition: 2001–10*, 39.

111. Ibid., 38.

112. Ibid., 50.

113. Ibid., 52.

114. Ibid., 37.

115. Correra, *MI6*, 340.

116. Ibid., 333.

117. https://api.parliament.uk/historic-hansard/commons/2002/jan/21/british-detainees-guantanamo-bay#S6CV0378P0_20020121_HOC_165; https://www.theyworkforyou.com/wrans/?id=2002-01-09.24938.h; https://publications.parliament.uk/pa/cm200102/cmhansrd/vo020214/debtext/20214-12.htm.

118. https://www.counterpunch.org/2002/12/27/an-open-letter-to-president-bush-on-the-torture-of-al-qaeda-suspects/.

119. Blakeley, Ruth, and Sam Raphael, "British Torture in the 'War on

Terror,'" *European Journal of International Relations*, vol. 23, no. 2 (2017), 249.

120. *Detainee Mistreatment and Rendition*, 21.

121. Ibid., 131.

122. For instance, see the impressive work by Ruth Blakeley, Sam Raphael, and others on the Rendition Project: https://www.therenditionproject.org.uk/about/index.html.

123. https://www.businessinsider.com/snowden-leaks-timeline-2016-9?r=UK&IR=T.

124. http://www.spiegel.de/international/europe/british-spy-agency-gchq-hacked-belgian-telecoms-firm-a-923406.html.

125. MacAskill, Ewen, and others, "GCHQ taps fibre-optic cables for secret access to world's communications," *Guardian*, June 21, 2013.

126. Ibid.

127. For a full list of the challengers, see https://www.amnesty.org.uk/press-releases/campaigners-win-vital-battle-against-uk-mass-surveillance-european-court-human.

128. https://www.privacynotprism.org.uk/.

129. https://www.echr.coe.int/Documents/FS_Mass_surveillance_ENG.pdf

130. Omand and Phythian, *Principled Spying*, 153.

131. Omand and Phythian, *Principled Spying*, 155; Anderson, David, *A Question of Trust: Report of the Investigatory Powers Review* (London: Stationery Office, 2015).

132. ISC, *Privacy and Security: A Modern and Transparent Legal Framework* (London: Stationery Office, 2015), 58.

133. Omand and Phythian, *Principled Spying*, 155.

134. https://www.ipco.org.uk/docs/IPCO%20consulation%20on%20bulk%20powers%20-%20Liberty%20response%20June%202018.pdf.

135. https://www.reuters.com/article/us-amazon-com-jobs-automation-insight/amazon-scraps-secret-ai-recruiting-tool-that-showed-bias-against-women-idUSKCN1MK08G.

136. Hardy, Jack, "Torture witnesses come forward to help investigation into Army's IRA mole 'Stakeknife,'" *Telegraph*, 18 December 2018.

137. Evans, Rob, "Police spy should face charges for sexual relationship with activist, court told," *Guardian*, November 14, 2018.

138. Gayle, Damien, and Ian Cobain, "UK intelligence and police using child spies in covert operations," *Guardian*, July 19, 2018.

139. https://www.ipco.org.uk/docs/Juvenile%20CHIS%20March%208%202019.pdf.

Chapter 3

1. Former director general, Security Service. Interview with the author.

2. Former cabinet secretary. Interview with the author.

3. Former chair of the JIC. Interview with the author.

4. Former senior SIS officer. Interview with the author.
5. Former chief, SIS. Interview with the author.
6. Ibid.
7. Former cabinet secretary. Interview with the author.
8. Former member of the ISC. Interview with the author.
9. Former member of the ISC. Interview with the author.
10. Former director, GCHQ. Interview with the author.
11. Former national security advisor. Interview with the author.
12. Ibid.
13. Former director, GCHQ. Interview with the author.
14. Ibid.
15. Former national security advisor. Interview with the author.
16. Former director general of the Security Service. Interview with the author.
17. Former director, GCHQ. Interview with the author. The accounting officer is the senior civil servant in each agency.
18. Former national security advisor. Interview with the author.
19. Former senior SIS officer. Interview with the author.
20. Former security minister. Interview with the author.
21. Former director general of the Security Service. Interview with the author.
22. Former chair of the JIC. Interview with the author.
23. Ibid.
24. Former director of GCHQ. Interview with the author.
25. Former director of GCHQ. Interview with the author.
26. The author was unable to locate a specific editorial, but the interviewee may be referring to Jenkins, Sir Simon, "Edward Snowden has started a global debate. So why the silence in Britain?," *Guardian*, September 19, 2013.
27. ISC member. Interview with the author.
28. Former national security advisor. Interview with the author.
29. Former director general of the Security Service. Interview with the author.
30. Former senior SIS officer. Interview with the author.
31. Former director, GCHQ. Interview with the author.
32. Ibid.
33. Ibid.
34. Parker, Andrew, "MI5 chief security speech," *Telegraph*, October 8, 2013.
35. Former director general of the Security Service. Interview with the author.
36. Ibid.
37. Former director general of the Security Service. Interview with the author. See also Watts, Larry, "Intelligence Reform in Europe's Emerging Democracies," *Studies in Intelligence*, vol. 48, no. 1 (2007), 11–25.
38. Former senior SIS officer. Interview with the author.
39. Ethics counsellor. Interview with the author.

40. Former senior SIS officer. Interview with the author.

41. Ibid.

42. Former director general of the Security Service. Interview with the author.

43. Former director general of the Security Service. Interview with the author.

44. Ibid.

45. Former director, GCHQ. Interview with the author.

46. Former senior SIS officer. Interview with the author.

47. Former chief, SIS. Interview with the author.

48. Former senior SIS officer. Interview with the author.

49. Former director general of the Security Service. Interview with the author.

50. Ibid.

51. Former director general of the Security Service. Interview with the author.

52. Former senior SIS officer. Interview with the author.

53. Current practitioner. Interview with the author.

54. Former director general of the Security Service. Interview with the author.

55. Former national security advisor. Interview with the author.

56. Former director general of the Security Service. Interview with the author.

57. Ibid.

58. Former senior SIS officer. Interview with the author.

59. Former director general of the Security Service. Interview with the author.

60. Former chief of SIS. Interview with the author.

61. Former national security advisor. Interview with the author.

62. Former national security advisor. Interview with the author.

63. Former national security advisor. Interview with the author.

64. Former director general of the Security Service. Interview with the author.

65. Judith Ward was convicted of involvement in the M62 bus bombing in 1974 on the basis of forensic evidence. Her conviction was vacated on appeal in 1993.

66. Borrill, Rachel, "Judge reverses ruling on disclosing evidence," *Independent*, January 16, 1993.

67. Former director general of the Security Service. Interview with the author.

68. Bowcott, Owen, "What are secret courts and what do they mean for UK justice?," *Guardian*, June 14, 2013.

69. Attorney General's Office, *Attorney General's Guidelines on Disclosure for Investigators, Prosecutors, and Defense Practitioners* (London: Attorney General's Office, 2013).

70. Former national security advisor. Interview with the author.

71. Current official in an intelligence agency. Interview with the author.

72. Former director general of the Security Service. Interview with the author. For this reason, IPCO utilizes the expertise of a Technical Advisory Panel, whose members attend inspections and can understand and explain the implications of the agencies' use of technology.

73. Private information; former director general of the Security Service. Interview with the author.

74. Former director general of the Security Service. Interview with the author.

75. Former senior SIS officer. Interview with the author.

76. Hannigan, Robert, "Director GCHQ's speech at Stonewall Workplace Conference," *Leeds,* April 15, 2016.

77. Current official in an intelligence agency. Interview with the author.

78. Former senior SIS officer. Interview with the author.

79. Former director, GCHQ. Interview with the author.

80. Current official in an intelligence agency. Interview with the author.

81. Current intelligence official. Interview with the author.

82. Former national security advisor. Interview with the author.

Chapter 4

1. Former director general of the Security Service. Interview with the author.

2. Former senior SIS officer. Interview with the author.

3. Former national security advisor. Interview with the author.

4. Former cabinet secretary. Interview with the author.

5. Hague, William, "Securing Our Future," speech, November 16, 2011. https://www.gov.uk/government/speeches/securing-our-future--2. In an interview with the author, a former national security advisor estimated that the number of submissions to the foreign secretary would be "two or three a week."

6. IPCO, *Annual Report of the Investigatory Powers Commissioner 2017* (London: Stationery Office, 2019), 42.

7. Former member of the ISC. Interview with the author.

8. Former director, GCHQ. Interview with the author.

9. Former national security advisor. Interview with the author.

10. Former national security advisor. Interview with the author.

11. Hague, William, "Foreign Secretary Statement to the House of Commons—GCHQ," June 10, 2013. https://www.gchq.gov.uk/speech/foreign-secretarys-statement-house-commons-role-gchq.

12. Former national security advisor. Interview with the author.

13. Former national security advisor. Interview with the author.

14. Former senior SIS officer. Interview with the author.

15. IPCO, *Annual Report of the Investigatory Powers Commissioner 2017,* 35.

16. Hague, "Securing Our Future"; Hague, "Foreign Secretary Statement."

17. IPCO, *Annual Report of the Investigatory Powers Commissioner 2017*, 56.
18. Former director, GCHQ. Interview with the author.
19. Former national security advisor. Interview with the author.
20. Former security minister. Interview with the author.
21. Former national security advisor. Interview with the author.
22. Former national security advisor. Interview with the author.
23. Blitz, James, "Head of UK civil service confirms permanent dual role," *Financial Times*, February 14, 2019.
24. Former national security advisor. Interview with the author.
25. Younger, Alex, "Remarks by the Chief of the Secret Intelligence Service," Vauxhall Cross, December 8, 2016; Parker, Andrew, "MI5 chief security speech," *Telegraph*, October 9, 2013; Parker, Andrew, "Speech to BfV Symposium," Berlin, May 14, 2018.
26. Younger, "Remarks by the Chief of the Secret Intelligence Service."
27. Former national security advisor. Interview with the author.
28. Former member of the ISC. Interview with the author.
29. IPCO, *Annual Report of the Investigatory Powers Commissioner 2017*, 66.
30. IPCO staff member. Interview with the author.
31. Ibid., 12.
32. Ibid., 78.
33. Ibid., 75.
34. IPCO Inspector. Interview with the author.
35. Ibid.
36. Ibid., 23.
37. Ibid.
38. Former national security advisor. Interview with the author.
39. Grieve, Dominic. Sky News interview, November 2, 2019.
40. Haynes, Deborah. "Russia report row: Dominic Grieve accuses PM of using No 10 'to spread propaganda and disinformation,'" Sky News, November 6 2019. For the Hansard debates, go to: https://parliamentlive.tv/event/index/95d372d7-e8e9-431c-93ab-692c6b631a1b?in=12:35:15.
41. Former senior SIS officer. Interview with the author.
42. Former director, GCHQ. Interview with the author.
43. Former director general of the Security Service. Interview with the author.
44. Former chief, SIS. Interview with the author.
45. Former director general of the Security Service. Interview with the author.
46. Ibid.
47. Ibid.
48. Ibid.
49. Ibid.
50. IOCCO, *Report of the Interception of Communications Commissioner Annual Report for 2016* (London: Stationery Office, 2017), 38.

51. Ibid.
52. Former security minister. Interview with the author.
53. Former chief, SIS. Interview with the author.
54. Sawers, Sir John, "Conversations in Diplomacy: Sir John Sawers," March 1, 2018, Belfer Center, https://www.belfercenter.org/publication/conversations-diplomacy-sir-john-sawers.
55. Former director general of the Security Service. Interview with the author.
56. Former director, GCHQ. Interview with the author.
57. Parker, "MI5 chief security speech."
58. Former director, GCHQ. Interview with the author. This individual was adamant that an organization's responsiveness was not the same as accountability. However, this understanding was common among their peers as an important component of how accountability works in practice.
59. Bemelmans-Videc, Marie-Louise, Jeremy Lonsdale, and Burt Perrin, *Making Accountability Work: Dilemmas for Evaluation and for Audit* (London: Transaction, 2007).
60. Former director general of the Security Service. Interview with the author.
61. Former national security advisor. Interview with the author.
62. NSA, *Annex: Learning Lessons from the Iraq Inquiry: The National Security Adviser's Report*, January 1, 2017, https://publications.parliament.uk/pa/cm201719/cmselect/cmpubadm/708/70803.htm.
63. Former chief, SIS. Interview with the author.
64. NSA, *Annex: Learning Lessons.*
65. Current intelligence officer. Interview with the author.
66. Former director, GCHQ. Interview with the author.
67. Former senior SIS officer. Interview with the author.
68. Ethics counsellor. Interview with the author.
69. Andrew, Christopher, *The Defence of the Realm*: *The Authorised History of MI5* (London: Penguin, 2009).
70. Younger, Alex, "Inside the Modern Day MI6," December 8, 2016.
71. Former director general of the Security Service. Interview with the author.
72. Ibid.
73. Ibid.
74. Ibid.
75. Ibid.
76. Ibid.
77. ISC, *Annual Report 2007–08* (London: Stationery Office, 2008), 19.
78. Former director, GCHQ. Interview with the author.
79. Former director, GCHQ. Interview with the author.
80. Former director, GCHQ. Interview with the author.

81. Former director, GCHQ. Interview with the author.
82. Ibid.
83. Ethics counsellor. Interview with the author.
84. Ibid.
85. Ibid.
86. Current practitioner. Interview with the author.
87. Ethics counsellor. Interview with the author.
88. Current intelligence officer. Interview with the author.
89. Hannigan, Robert, "Director GCHQ's speech at Stonewall Workplace Conference," April 15, 2016.
90. ISC member. Interview with the author.
91. Former national security advisor. Interview with the author.
92. Former director general of the Security Service. Interview with the author.

Chapter 5

1. Lobban, Iain, "Speech in Tribute to Alan Turing," *Leeds,* October 4, 2012.
2. Former senior SIS officer. Interview with the author.
3. Former director, GCHQ. Interview with the author.
4. Hague, William, "Securing Our Future," speech, November 16, 2011.
5. Norton-Taylor, Richard, "Binyam Mohamed torture evidence must be revealed, judges rule," *Guardian*, February 10, 2010.
6. Former member of the ISC. Interview with the author.
7. Former national security advisor. Interview with the author.
8. Gaskarth, J., "Entangling Alliances? The U.K.'s Complicity in Torture in the Global War on Terrorism," *International Affairs*, vol. 87, no. 4 (2011), 945–64.
9. Lander, Sir Stephen, "International Intelligence Cooperation: An Insider's Perspective," in *Secret Intelligence: A Reader*, edited by Christopher Andrew, Richard J. Aldrich, and Wesley K. Wark (London: Routledge, 2009); Wetzling, Thorsten, "European Counterterrorism Intelligence Liaisons," in *PSI Handbook of Global Security and Intelligence: National Approaches*, edited by Stuart Farson, Peter Gill, Mark Phythian, and Shlomo Shpiro (London: Praeger, 2008), 1–40.
10. Former senior SIS officer. Interview with the author.
11. Ibid.
12. Mulholland, Hélène, Peter Walker, and agencies "BAE inquiry decision faces legal challenge," *Guardian*, December 15, 2006.
13. Former high commissioner to Pakistan. Interview with the author.
14. European Parliament Directorate for Internal Affairs, "The Results of Inquiries into the CIA's Program of Extraordinary Rendition and Secret Prisons in European States in Light of the New Legal Framework Following the Lisbon Treaty," http://www.europarl.europa.eu/RegData/etudes/note/join/2012/462456/IPOL-LIBE_NT%282012%29462456_EN.pdf, 61.

15. Former national security advisor. Interview with the author.

16. Ibid.

17. UN, *Report of the Special Rapporteur on the Promotion and Protection of Human Rights and Fundamental Freedoms while Countering Terrorism.* A/HRC/34/61, Human Rights Council, February 21, 2017.

18. http://assembly.coe.int/nw/xml/XRef/Xref-XML2HTML-en.asp?fileid=11527&lang=e.n.

19. http://assembly.coe.int/nw/xml/News/News-View-EN.asp?newsid=1918&lang=2.

20. https://www.un.org/press/en/2005/gashc3830.doc.htm.

21. http://assembly.coe.int/nw/xml/News/News-View-en.asp?newsid=5722&lang=2.

22. Current intelligence official. Interview with the author.

23. Private information.

24. Cormac, Rory, *Disrupt and Deny: Spies, Special Forces, and the Secret Pursuit of British Foreign Policy* (Oxford University Press, 2018), 264.

25. https://fas.org/sgp/crs/intel/RL33715.pdf, 1.

26. Cormac, *Disrupt and Deny*, 261.

27. Ibid., 233.

28. Ibid., 261.

29. Former senior SIS officer. Interview with the author.

30. Former director general of the Security Service. Interview with the author.

31. Former director, GCHQ. Interview with the author.

32. Former director, GCHQ. Interview with the author.

33. Former director, GCHQ. Interview with the author.

34. Former director, GCHQ. Interview with the author.

35. Former director, GCHQ. Interview with the author.

36. Bellamy, A., "No Pain, No Gain? Torture and Ethics in the War on Terror," *International Affairs*, vol. 82, no. 1 (January 2006), 121–48.

37. Former senior SIS officer. Interview with the author.

38. Margaret Beckett, foreign secretary 2006–07. Interview with the author, 2010.

39. Ibid.

40. Parker, Andrew, "Speech to BfV Symposium," Berlin, May 14, 2018.

41. Former national security advisor. Interview with the author.

42. Parker, "Speech to BfV Symposium."

43. Indeed, this applies to oversight bodies, too, with organizations like IPCO and the ISC engaging in extensive liaison and cooperation with their opposite numbers among the Five Eyes states and the group of five signatories to the common statement of Bern, namely: Belgium, Denmark, the Netherlands, Norway, and Switzerland, including attending conferences, conducting visits, and sharing expertise.

44. Former security minister. Interview with the author.
45. Former director general of the Security Service. Interview with the author.
46. Rt Hon Margaret Beckett, MP. Interview with the author.

Conclusion

1. Aldrich, Richard J., and Daniela Richterova, "Ambient Accountability: Intelligence Services in Europe and the Decline of State Secrecy," *West European Politics,* vol. 41, no. 4 (2018), 2.
2. The UK intelligence services were aware of a threat from al-Qaeda in the runup to 9/11, but did not know where the attacks were to take place. Correra, Gordon, *MI6* (London: Weidenfeld and Nicolson, 2011), 330.
3. Former director, GCHQ. Interview with the author.
4. Former national security advisor. Interview with the author.
5. NSA, Lessons Learned.
6. Ministry of Defence, *Global Strategic Trends: The Future Starts Today.*
7. Gaskarth, "UK Complicity in Torture."
8. https://www.aclu.org/cases/senate-torture-report-foia.
9. https://www.ipco.org.uk/docs/IPCO%20Consultation%20on%20the%20Consolidated%20Guidance.pdf; ISC, *Detainee Mistreatment and Rendition: Current Issues* (London: Stationery Office, 2018).
10. https://www.theguardian.com/uk-news/2018/jun/02/uk-spies-breaching-rules-sharing-intelligence-gained-torture-mi5-mi6.
11. Former chief, SIS. Interview with the author.
12. Sandel, M., *What Money Can't Buy: The Moral Limits of Markets* (London: Penguin, 2013).
13. Younger, "Remarks by the Chief of the Secret Intelligence Service."
14. Ibid.
15. https://www.hra.nhs.uk/planning-and-improving-research/policies-standards-legislation/governance-arrangement-research-ethics-committees/.
16. Al-Shahi, R., "Research Ethics Committees in the U.K.—The Pressure Is Now on Research and Development Departments," *Journal of the Royal Society of Medicine*, vol. 98, no. 10 (October 2005), 444–47.
17. Former chief, SIS. Interview with the author.
18. Former director, GCHQ. Interview with the author.
19. Former national security advisor. Interview with the author.

Index

www.ingramcontent.com/pod-product-compliance
Ingram Content Group UK Ltd.
Pitfield, Milton Keynes, MK11 3LW, UK
UKHW041101150926
475561UK00002BA/40

9 780815 737971